EXPRESSIONS UNBOUND

AMERICAN OUTSIDER ART

TUFTS UNIVERSITY ART GALLERIES
TISCH FAMILY GALLERY, AIDEKMAN ARTS CENTER
MEDFORD, MASSACHUSETTS

EXPRESSIONS UNBOUND

AMERICAN OUTSIDER ART

FROM THE

ANDREW AND LINDA SAFRAN

COLLECTION

Contents

Director's Foreword

A university's art collection—like any collection—is a reflection of the institution's aspirations. Since the nineteenth century, Tufts University has benefitted from the generosity of the community it has built through alumni, scholars, and supporters who have crossed its distinguished halls. Moreover, because Tufts is a research university, our collection reflects the rigor and goals of our academics—of teaching culture through its visual expression, from the very latest images to the earliest artifacts.

The thirty-eight artworks that comprise the Andrew and Linda Safran Collection mark an unprecedented moment for Tufts University's Permanent Art Collection. It is the first large-scale contribution of American outsider art to the school—expanding our holdings in an area that has seen notable scholarly growth in the past decade. This significant gift of works largely by African American artists allows us to continue the project of opening the canon of art history, not only to a more inclusive global history, but also to a localized, national history that speaks to the divides in class, race, and educational opportunity that our field has unwittingly reinforced. These paintings, sculptures, and drawings by renowned self-taught artists such as Thornton Dial, Mary T. Smith, William L. Hawkins, and Purvis Young join our existing holdings of works by Elaine de Kooning, Helen Frankenthaler, Alice Neel, Louise Nevelson, John Singer Sargent, Andy Warhol, and Grant Wood, fueling the research by the next generation of scholars that will yield a nuanced, richer narrative of twentieth-century American art.

For this extraordinary opportunity, I extend my deepest gratitude to collectors Andrew and Linda Safran, who so generously shared their vision of art and creative practice with us. This gift epitomizes their extensive engagement with Tufts, and we are honored to continue their legacy through the exhibitions programs and the arts on campus. The Tufts University Art Galleries are proud to present this catalogue as a record of the entire Safran gift and its accompanying exhibition. We are indebted to art historian Evie T. Joselow, PhD, for authoring this work of scholarship with true dedication to and passion for the field.

This presentation marks just the beginning of what we hope will be a deep and ongoing engagement with American outsider art for years to come.

Dina Deitsch, Director, Chief Curator
Tufts University Art Galleries

Expressions Unbound—American Outsider Art

Artistic works such as paintings, drawings, statues, and statuettes, various objects of all sorts, owing nothing (or as little as possible) to the imitation of art that one can see in museums, salons, and galleries, but that on the contrary appeal to humanity's first origins and the most spontaneous personal invention; works which the artist has entirely derived (invention and manner of expression) from his own sources, from his own impulses and humors, without regard for the rules for current convention.

—Jean Dubuffet, "Notice sur la Compagnie de l'Art Brut," September 1948 [1]

The idea of innovative artistic forms of expression, created independently and outside the boundaries of accepted cultural conventions in twentieth-century art, was first posited by the avant-garde French artist Jean Dubuffet. It became the guiding principle of the *Compagnie de l'Art Brut*, 1948, and the Art Brut movement (translated as "Raw Art").[2] As explained by Roger Cardinal in his seminal book, *Outsider Art* (1972), Dubuffet—using the term Art Brut—sought to find an alternative mode of art, focusing on original and authentic work that conveys "what grows naturally and is projected naturally from the psychic depths of the artist."[3] Cardinal first coined the term "outsider art," identifying and defining a group of "untutored" European "artists outside culture," many suffering from mental illness, who expressed their own emotional terrain of experiences through unconventional norms.[4] In American art history, attributes of Art Brut became better known as outsider art, focusing on a wider range of self-taught artists marginalized from mainstream artistic traditions for various other circumstances.[5]

The Safran Collection showcases a group of outsider artists, each with his or her own personal style, themes, and iconography. These instructive and informative works broadly reflect the artists' own beliefs, fantasies, and life experiences, "bearing witness to an obvious inventiveness and independence."[6] Through their art we, the viewers, bear witness to their lives, their inspirations, resourcefulness, and keen perceptions from different environments and geographic locations. We also get a glimpse of their personal struggles and demons, demonstrating their perseverance in all kinds of situations to find unique, creative ways and means of expression.

In so looking and seeking, we find both ordinary and extraordinary human traits and special characteristics. Some were drawn to art at early ages (David Butler and Jimmy Lee Sudduth), having limited access to materials. But many others discovered their artistic calling later in their lives, finding new expressive outlets to tell stories about their experiences and aspirations. Most were working men and women, some married with families, or some sort of ties to their communities or a geographic locale. Their everyday occupations included long stints as vocational tradesmen for big industrial concerns: Thornton Dial was a metalworker for the Pullman-Standard Company; Sanford Darling worked as an engineer at General Petroleum; and Benjamin (B. F.) Perkins was a US Marine, serving on a security detail at the White House. They were farmers (Raymond Coins worked on his family's tobacco farm), coal miners (John "Jack" Savitsky), woodworkers and furniture makers (David Butler and Mose Tolliver), and a domestic worker (Mary T. Smith). Howard Finster and B. F. Perkins also found religion, creating inspirational "home-grown" art to reflect their preaching words. However, upon closer examination, their creative work was also informed by the other more eclectic outside jobs they pursued in their lives. Sanford Darling worked as a Hollywood stuntman, a commercial fisherman, and a chiropractor. Thornton Dial was a housepainter, commercial fisherman, and pipe fitter; and William L. Hawkins worked as a trapper, truck driver, scrap metal dealer, and ran a brothel, among other odd jobs. When he was not preaching, Howard Finster supplemented his income by working as a plumber, bicycle and television repairman, taxidermist, and carpenter.[7]

With the exception of Justin McCarthy and Malcolm McKesson, who were born into well-to-do families, many of the artists struggled with the burdens of poverty, which further marginalized them from society. Thornton Dial buried "found" materials in his yard, believing that he needed a license to make things that he could not afford.[8] The impoverished lives of the artists made it virtually impossible for many to receive formal artistic training, leading them to invent materials (Jimmy Lee Sudduth's "mud mixtures"), to scavenge and recycle (Thornton Dial and David Butler), to use any available interior or exterior wall surfaces (Sanford Darling, Howard Finster, B. F. Perkins, and Purvis Young), as well as to rely upon hardware-store variety products including household paint, cardboard, plywood, Masonite, and metal (David Butler, Thornton Dial, William L. Hawkins, Mary T. Smith, and Purvis Young). Others, like Raymond Coins and Bessie Harvey, foraged in nature, using found stones and wood pieces, including broken tree limbs; both allowed the shape of the natural material, in part, to determine the imagery they produced—he for his "doll babies" and she for her "spirit-realm" artifacts.[9] Still others drew inspiration directly from the scenery and figures of the local and urban landscape, documenting everyday life as well as imaginary encounters. Thornton Dial's works evoked the experiences of African American life in the South; Jack Savitsky revisited the coal country of Pennsylvania; and Purvis Young documented the turmoil and violence of urban life, as well as his own fictional battles with horses, police, and guns.[10] Mental illness and other physical and social disabilities also played a defining role in the creation of distinctive artistic visions in closed environments—in confinement (Ray Hamilton), in secrecy (Malcolm McKesson), working behind closed doors and screened windows (Sanford Darling and David Butler), and in their own transformative states (Charles Benefiel).[11]

Attracted by the notion of creating their own "triumphant personal visions," and desiring to find a space and place to share their artistic passions, Sanford Darling, Howard Finster, and B. F. Perkins all created their own visionary built-environments.[12] Sanford Darling's "House of a 1,000 Paintings" became a local landmark in Santa Barbara, California, drawing more than eight thousand visitors.[13] Both Mary T. Smith and Mose Tolliver displayed art in their front yards—her outdoor portrait gallery could be seen from the nearby highway, and his paintings, propped up and hung from tree limbs, both attracted sales and stimulated his own production.[14] David Butler made his presence known, riding around his neighborhood on a painted bicycle with mechanical flourishes of his own making.[15]

While many of the artists independently created in isolated environments, and most of the time without a specific audience in mind, some held aspirations for public recognition.[16] William L. Hawkins collected popular culture imagery, cut out of magazines, newspapers, and advertisements, which he kept archived and in a suitcase hidden under his bed.[17] Justin McCarthy, an avid television watcher, captured screen-shots and still images of celebrities.[18] Howard Finster became a celebrity in his own right, making several late-night television appearances on the Johnny Carson show and exhibiting two works at the Venice Biennale (1984), as well as designing album covers for the rock-and-roll groups R.E.M and the Talking Heads.[19] Purvis Young gained recognition as an acclaimed street artist in *Purvis of Overtown* (2006), a documentary film that followed his transition from incarceration to a notable career painting wall murals in the Overtown neighborhood of Miami.[20]

Several artists in the Safran Collection have also been included in pivotal museum exhibitions featuring self-taught artists, thereby entering into the mainstream of art historical study and interpretation, and earning "the credentials and validation used to identify, characterize and classify artifacts and their makers."[21] Bessie Harvey was the first black woman to be represented in the *Whitney Biennial* (1995).[22] Justin McCarthy's work appeared in *Seventeen Naïve Painters*, organized by the Museum of Modern Art, New York (1966–67). Works by David Butler and Mose Tolliver were included in the seminal exhibition *Black Folk Art in America* (1982), at the Corcoran Gallery, Washington, DC, and Charles Benefiel's work was featured in *Obsessive Drawing* at the American Folk Art Museum, New York (2006). Thornton Dial's works have been included in many important solo and group exhibitions, including *Thornton Dial, Image of the Tiger*, at the American Folk Art Museum and the New Museum of Contemporary Art, New York (1993–94); the *Whitney Biennial*, Whitney Museum of American Art, New York (2000); and a second major museum solo exhibition, *Thornton Dial in the 21st Century* at the Museum of Fine Arts, Houston (2005). This year ushers in two major exhibitions featuring outsider artists. *Outliers and the American Vanguard*, at the National Gallery of Art, Washington, DC (January 28–May 13, 2018, and traveling), presents a new discourse between established artists and those with different backgrounds and approaches, "with respect to artistic training, tradition, class, race, ethnicity, gender and mental or developmental disability."[23] *History Refused to Die: Highlights from the Souls Grown Deep Foundation*, at the Metropolitan Museum of Art, New York (May 22–September 23, 2018), highlights thirty works by artists from the American South, including Thornton Dial, from a collection recently gifted to the museum.[24]

Whether embedded in worlds of their own creation, inspired by chance, or motivated by circumstance, what is clear is that through different ways and means the artists in the Safran Collection found their own unique expressive outlets, to spontaneously and freely create with a minimum of interference from others during the creative process.[25] As succinctly summarized by Purvis Young: "I didn't know no one was gonna see 'em or want to buy 'em. I did it because I wanted to express my feelin's about the world."[26]

Evie T. Joselow, PhD

1. Lucienne Peiry, *Art Brut: The Origins of Outsider Art* (Paris: Flammarion, 2001), 11; from "Notice sur la Compagnie de l'Art Brut," September 1948 (Archives of the Collection de l'Art Brut, Lausanne); text reprinted in *Prospectus et tous écrits suivants*, vol. 1 (Paris: Gallimard, 1967), 489–91.
2. Ibid., 11.
3. Roger Cardinal, *Outsider Art* (New York: Praeger Publishers, 1972), 24.
4. Ibid., 7. Cardinal is Professor Emeritus, University of Kent, England.
5. Lynne Cooke, "Boundary Trouble: Navigating Margin and Mainstream," in *Outliers and American Vanguard Art* (Washington, DC: National Gallery of Art and the University of Chicago Press, 2018), 14. This essay offers a chronological paradigm of the evolution of thinking in American art circles, from 1924 to 2013, starting with a rethinking of the folk art aesthetic, and encompassing a new category of contemporary "outliers."
6. Peiry, *Art Brut*, 11.
7. Frank Maresca, Roger Ricco, with Lyle Rexer, *American Self-Taught: Paintings and Drawings by Outsider Artists* (New York: Alfred A. Knopf, 1993), 72.
8. Kathy Moses, *Outsider Art of the South* (Atglen, PA: Schiffer, 1999), 148. Dial's children joked that his property sat "higher than the neighbors because of the layers of decomposed works and projects beneath." Robert Bishop, "Thornton Dial: An Ordinary and Unique American Artist," in *Thornton Dial, Strategy of the World*, William S. Arnett and Paul Arnett (Jamaica, NY: Southern Queens Park Association / African American Hall of Fame, 1990), 3.
9. Gail Andrews Treschel, ed. *Pictured in My Mind: Contemporary American Self-Taught Art from the Collection of Dr. Kurt Gitter and Alice Rae Yelen* (Birmingham, AL: Birmingham Museum of Art and University Press of Mississippi, 1995), 44. According to Bessie Harvey, "God had shown her how to locate the spiritual presence in nature—to draw figures and faces so that she could talk to them and be comforted." Moses, *Outsider Art of the South*, 88.
10. The horse is a recurring motif in Purvis Young's works, with wild black horses symbolizing freedom, and white stallions representing oppression. Moses, *Outsider Art of the South*, 202.
11. Cardinal, *Outsider Art*, 29. Charles Benefiel's repetitive drawings could be viewed as "a reformative function of artistic expression," a notion raised by Cardinal and based on the thinking of Dr. Leo Navratil, an early twentieth-century Viennese doctor who studied schizophrenic patients, as well as thoughts espoused by André Breton, an artist also tied to Art Brut. Cardinal writes, "the art of those who are mentally ill constitutes a reservoir of moral health . . . whereby the mechanisms of artistic creation are freed of all impediment" (21).
12. Steven C. Dubin, "The Centrality of Marginality: Naïve Artists and Savvy Supporters," in *Outsider Art: Contesting Boundaries in Contemporary Culture*, ed. Vera Zolberg and Joni Maya Cherbo (New York: Cambridge University Press, 1997), 39.
13. Ibid., 49.
14. According to Frank Maresca and Roger Ricco, for Smith, "tidying up her yard meant displaying paintings to encourage visitors." Maresca and Ricco, *American Self-Taught*, 240. They also write, "When one [painting] sold [Tolliver] would often duplicate the subject, soon establishing a theme with variations" for yet another sale (220).
15. Alice Rae Yelen, *Passionate Visions of the American South: Self-Taught Artists from 1940 to the Present* (New Orleans: New Orleans Museum of Art and University Press of Mississippi, 1993), 67.
16. Peiry, *Art Brut*, 11.
17. Hawkins also noted, "You have to do something wonderful, so people know who you are." Maresca and Ricco, *American Self-Taught*, 89.
18. For McCarthy, "art seems to have served not only as a means of expression, but also as a way of reforging and sustaining his links with the world." Ibid., 142.
19. Ibid., 74.
20. *Purvis of Overtown*, directed by David Raccuglia and Shaun Conrad (Rural Studios, 2006). The film features Purvis Young, William Arnett, Jane Fonda, and the collectors Donald and Mera Rubell.
21. Cooke, "Boundary Trouble," 3.
22. Moses, *Outsider Art of the South*, 88.
23. Earl A. Powell, III, "Director's Foreword," in Cooke, *Outliers and American Vanguard Art*, vii. The exhibition includes works by David Butler and Howard Finster and will travel to the High Museum of Art, Atlanta (June 24–September 30, 2018), and to the Los Angeles County Museum of Art (November 18, 2018–March 18, 2019).
24. The exhibition is accompanied by the catalogue *My Soul Has Grown Deep: Black Art from the American South* (New Haven: Metropolitan Museum of Art and Yale University Press, 2018), with essays by Cheryl Finely, Randall R. Griffey, Amelia Peck, and Darryl Pinckney.
25. Peiry, *Art Brut*, 11.
26. Moses, *Outsider Art of the South*, 200.

The Collection

It has been a joy collecting and studying American outsider art and artists over the past three decades. We are delighted that this collection is now part of the Tufts University Permanent Art Collection, to be studied and enjoyed by this community and so many others in the coming years.

We started this collection in 1989 with the acquisition of our first painting, *Hippo* by William L. Hawkins. We were captivated by the vibrant use of color and the simplicity of the subject in this large-scale artwork. We immediately wanted to know everything about the artist and his work. It was at this time that we began to learn about American outsider art. For the next eleven years we continued to expand our collection while attending art fairs, visiting galleries, and viewing exhibitions. The paintings, drawings, and sculptures we acquired were often created by making use of available materials, by drawing upon life experiences and recollections of the artists, and by interacting with personal environments.

We hope that viewing and interacting with this collection will not only inspire curiosity and engender an appreciation for the simplicity of the images and forms, but will help new audiences understand that this artwork speaks volumes about the complexity of these artists' talents and passions.

Andrew and Linda Safran

Charles BENEFIEL

(AMERICAN, B. 1967)

UNTITLED, N.D.
MIXED MEDIA AND STENCILS ON HANDMADE PAPER
23 × 15 IN.
2017.001

Charles Benefiel, born in Venice Beach, California, presently lives and works in San Diego. Diagnosed with obsessive-compulsive disorder in his adulthood, Benefiel took up drawing as a means of controlling and minimizing his anxieties and addressing trauma stemming from an early childhood accident.[1] His work includes both pictorial and numerical imagery. In his drawings he creates his own schematic language, using a Radiograph technical pen to repetitively render minuscule dots, a technique known as stippling. As Benefiel draws, he counts the dots, formulating his own continuous sequence of numbers before starting to count again. Such a process enables him to "chain his mind" and focus his thoughts on the act of creating.[2] He begins his constructed compositions from the center or works left to right, without any preliminary design in mind, but with a predetermined direction. His drawings are often finished with a stain of tea and varnish, "to evoke the qualities of time and timelessness."[3]

In this mixed-media work from his number series, Benefiel's dots cohere into a cryptic, numerical language. This work exemplifies his repeating and patterned rows of seemingly endless circles and dots, mimicking the appearance of a typewritten text, while creating his own abstract notations.

---

1. Julian Stern, "Accidental Magic," *Brut Force*, March 4, 2015, http://brutforce.com/accidental-magic/.
2. Bernard L. Herman, "Charles Benefiel," *Raw Vision* 30 (Spring 2000): 32. "Drawing the numbers in continuous sequence provided a means for containing the forces that controlled his life" (33).
3. According to Herman, the staining process is also repetitive and arduous, and "stems from looking at old family photographs." Ibid., 32.

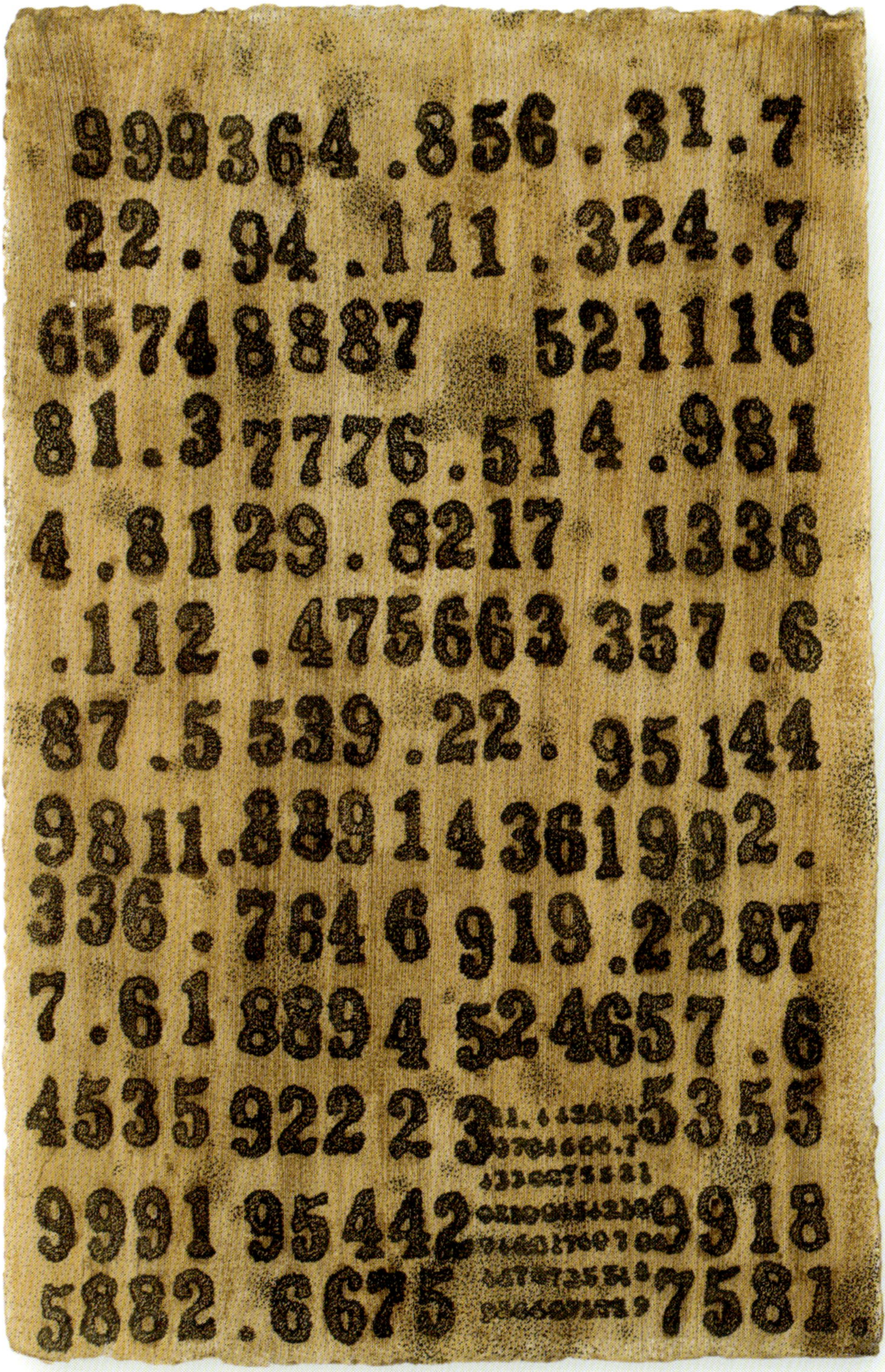
999364.856.31.7
22.94.111.324.7
65748887 .521116
81.37776.514.981
4.8129.8217 .1336
.112.475663 357.6
87.5539.22. 95144
9811.88914361992.
336.7646919.2287
7.61889 4 524657.6
4535 9222 3 5355
999195442 9918
5882.6675 7581.

David BUTLER

(AMERICAN, 1898-1997)

David Butler was born on the outskirts of Patterson, Louisiana. At an early age he began carving scenes and animals he saw around him, as a means of entertaining his seven younger siblings while his parents worked. Following in his father's footsteps, Butler also became a woodworker at a local sawmill. His art career commenced in his early forties, following a debilitating injury at the mill. Working primarily with readily available household and enamel paints and salvaged metal pieces, Butler began to create an imaginative world in his own yard, crafting fantastical cutout and kinetic sculptures of colorfully painted and patterned exotic creatures, farm animals, and other invented forms. He also covered the windows of his house with sheets of perforated tin as a form of spiritual protection, referring to the pieces as "spirit shields."[1] Butler became a well-known figure in his local community for the unique, multi-colored domestic environment he created, as well as for his excursions around town on a decorated bicycle that functioned as a kinetic sculpture.[2]

Salmon, *Heart*, and *Rooster* represent his signature method of creating art from corrugated tin roofing panels. After flattening and cutting the metal, Butler would embellish the surface with bold colors and patterns that are whimsical and decorative, as well as personally meaningful and spiritually protective.

SALMON, N.D.
PAINTED, CUT SHEET METAL,
ON CUSTOM METAL WALL MOUNT
RECTO/VERSO
12 × 26 IN.
2017.002

HEART, N.D.
PAINTED, CUT SHEET METAL,
ON CUSTOM METAL WALL MOUNT
RECTO/VERSO
7 × 11 IN.
2017.003

ROOSTER, 1985
PAINTED, CUT SHEET METAL,
ON CUSTOM METAL STAND
RECTO/VERSO
19 × 27 × 9 IN.
2017.004

---

1. Maude Southwell Wahlman, "Spirit Shields," in *Souls Grown Deep: African American Vernacular Art of the South*, vol. 2, *Once That River Starts to Flow*, ed. Paul Arnett and William Arnett (Atlanta: Tinwood Books, 2001), 140–47.
2. Lauren Palmor, "David Butler," in *Revelations: Art from the African American South*, ed. Timothy Anglin Burgard (San Francisco: Fine Arts Museums of San Francisco, de Young, and DelMonico Books, Prestel, 2017), 171. For further description of the bicycle, see Alice Rae Yelen, *Passionate Visions of the American South: Self-Taught Artists from 1940 to the Present* (New Orleans: New Orleans Museum of Art and University Press of Mississippi, 1993), 67.

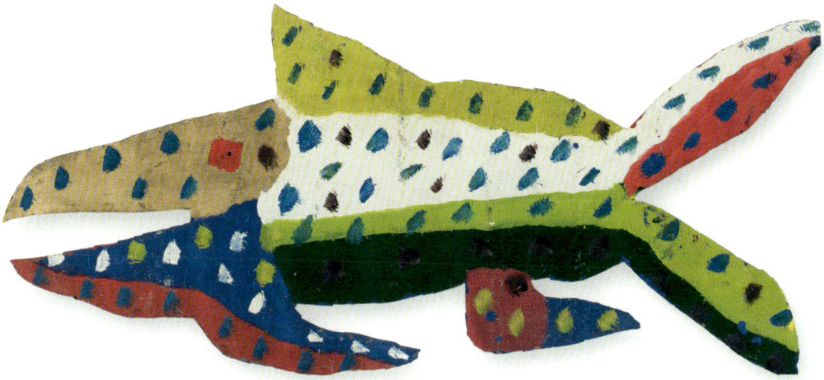

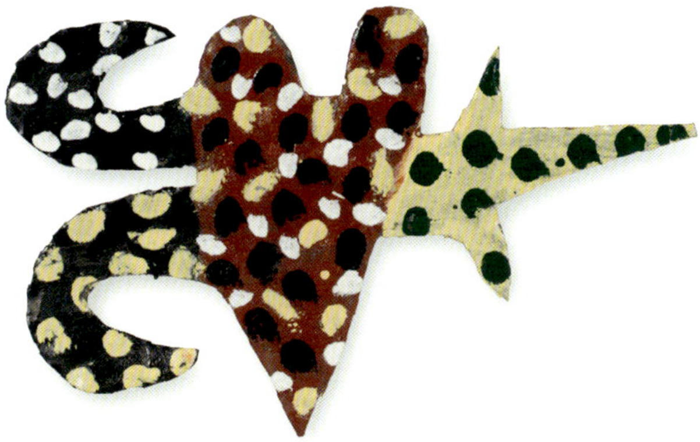

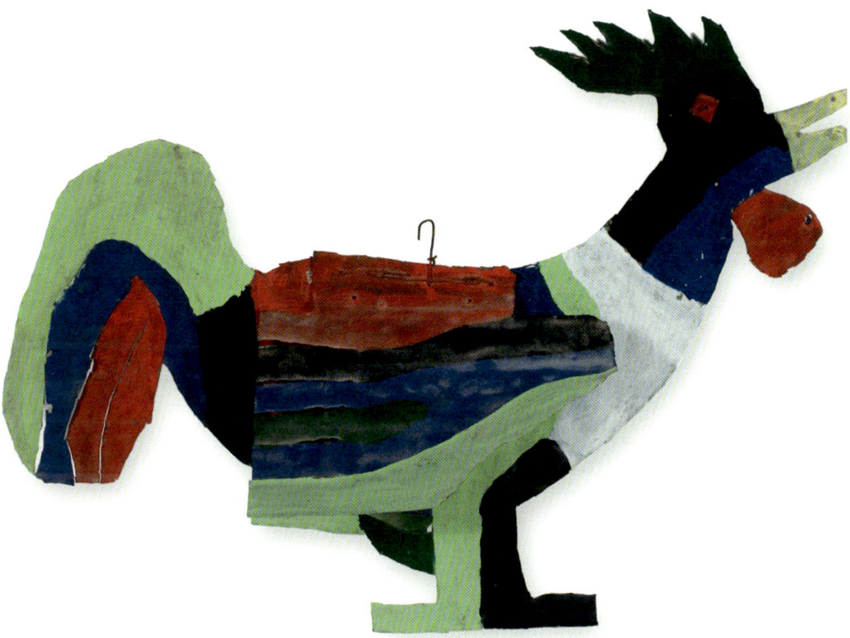

Raymond COINS

(AMERICAN, 1904–1998)

IN GOD WE TUST [SIC], N.D.
RELIEF IN STONE
(RIVER STONE)
20 × 12 × 3 IN.
2017.005

STATUE OF LIBERTY, N.D.
RELIEF IN STONE
(RIVER STONE)
17 × 8½ × 2½ IN.
2017.006

Raymond Coins was born in Stuart, Virginia. He left school in the fifth grade and spent much of his life near Winston-Salem, North Carolina, working on his family's tobacco farm. Upon his retirement in 1976, Coins took up stone and wood carving as a hobby, initially in imitation of Native American artifacts.[1] Working with natural materials, he quickly found his own unique style, creating figural sculptures and reliefs ranging in scale from small to nearly life-size. Coins stressed the intuitive quality of his process, carving figures he envisioned in the raw material, and making them fit and follow the contours of his locally found materials, including soapstone, river stone, and discarded wood.[2] His best-known works are his figural stone sculptures, which he referred to as "baby dolls."[3]

In God We Tust [*sic*] exemplifies Coins's deep interest in patriotic and religious themes. Coins was a devout member of a Primitive Baptist congregation and believed that personal guidance from God came to him in dreams and visions.[4] In *Statue of Liberty*, the iconic American monument is rendered with shallow carving and minimal detail, but is immediately recognizable.

---

1. Tom Patterson, "Raymond Coins," in *Pictured in My Mind: Contemporary American Self-Taught Art from the Collection of Dr. Kurt Gitter and Alice Rae Yelen*, ed. Gail Andrews Treschel (Birmingham, AL: Birmingham Museum of Art and University Press of Mississippi, 1995), 43.
2. Ibid., 38.
3. Ibid., 40.
4. "I was showed everything [by God] . . . and I've stuck to everything I've been shown." Ibid., 41.

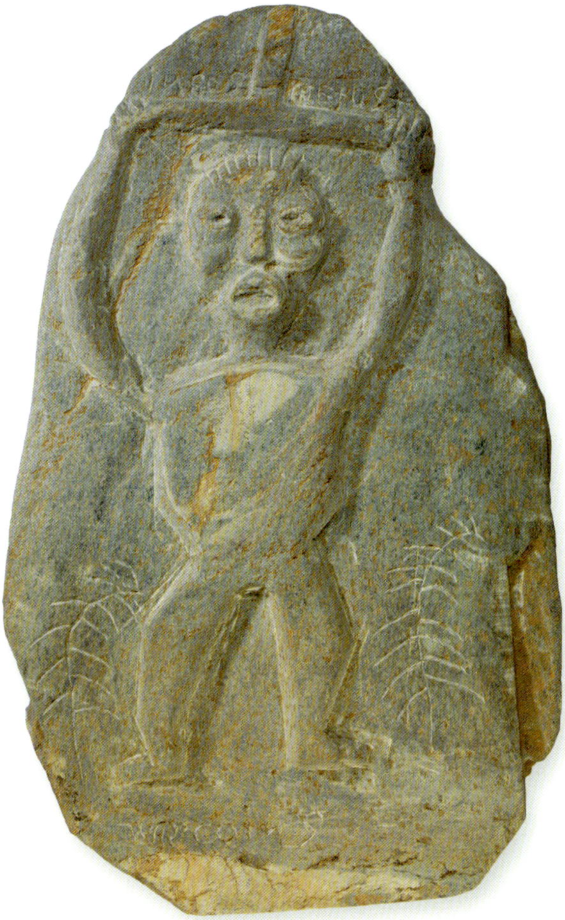

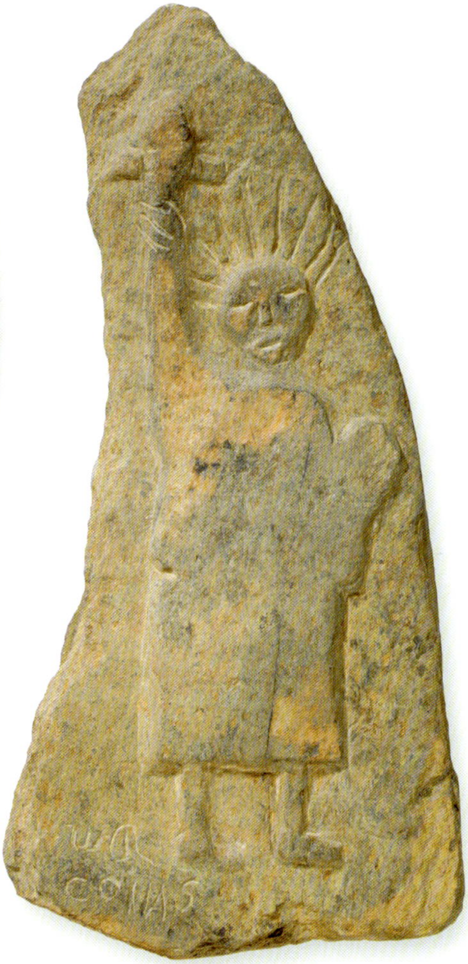

Sanford DARLING

(AMERICAN, 1894–1973)

UNTITLED, N.D.
POLYCHROME ON PLYWOOD
33½ × 15 IN.
2017.007

Born in Santa Barbara, California, Sanford Darling worked a variety of jobs throughout his life, including stints as a Hollywood stuntman, a fisherman, a chiropractor, and an engineer for General Petroleum. After his retirement, and the death of his wife, he embarked on two extended trips to Europe and Asia. When Darling returned to Santa Barbara in 1963 he turned his travel impressions and memories into an art form, transforming his house into a notable and colorful environment known as the "House of a 1,000 Paintings." Just about every interior and exterior surface—including walls, floors, windows, beams, and other architectural elements, as well as appliances and interior furnishings—was covered with brightly hued scenes and images reminiscent of his travels, as well as from his childhood. Darling found artistic inspiration in a range of real and imaginary landscapes: from palm tree–lined beaches to snowy mountains and castles along the Rhine. The home itself became a local landmark.[1]

This colorfully painted tropical scene featuring palm trees and a hut is a disassembled piece from the "House of a 1,000 Paintings." Painted in vivid greens and blues on a plywood board, tropical scenes such as this dotted the exterior entrance of Darling's house, with the steps to his front porch and doorframe patterned with the same motif.[2] Upon his death in 1973, Darling's "art environment" was disassembled, and paintings and other objects from the house were sold to private collectors.

1. Frank Maresca, Roger Ricco, with Lyle Rexer, *American Self-Taught: Paintings and Drawings by Outsider Artists* (New York: Alfred A. Knopf, 1993), 49.
2. For images of Darling's "House of a 1,000 Paintings," see Jo Farb Hernández, "Sanford Darling, House of a 1000 Paintings," *SPACES*, November 26, 2012, www.spacesarchives.org/explore/collection/environment/house-of-a-1000-paintings. As noted in the comment section by one local visitor, "Growing up in Santa Barbara, we used to visit this house every so often to gaze in awe; the owner was very friendly and generous at letting random visitors enter the house to look around. It had been gone for years before I heard about its demise. Quite sad; I wish I could have visited one final time, but at least I have the memories of it."

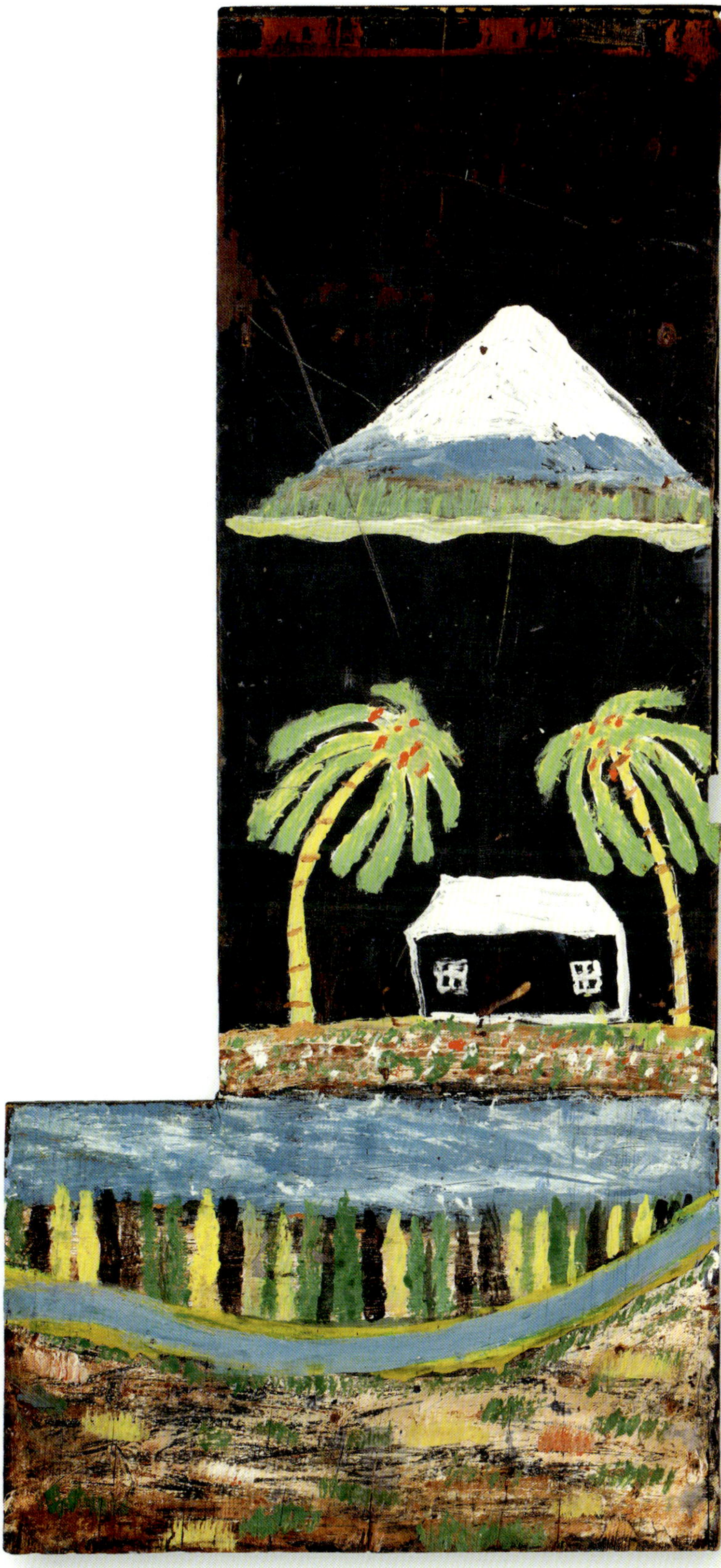

Thornton DIAL

(AMERICAN, 1928-2016)

EVERYDAY LIFE SERIES 1, 1993
WATERCOLOR AND MIXED MEDIA ON RAG PAPER
9½ × 12 IN.
2017.008

EVERYDAY LIFE SERIES 2, 1993
WATERCOLOR AND MIXED MEDIA ON RAG PAPER
12½ × 9 IN.
2017.009

Thornton Dial, also known as "Buck Dial," was born into a sharecropper family in Emelle, Alabama. He spent much of his life as a metalworker for the Pullman-Standard Company, and also took up various house trades—from painting and construction to fishing and pipe fitting—before devoting himself to art full time. Initially, Dial made art to please himself.[1] He created things clandestinely, burying or destroying some of his works for fear of discovery and unwanted attention.[2] For most of his life he was also unaware of the formal meaning of art. As a self-taught artist, he developed his own unique style and is best known for his sculptural objects and wall-relief assemblages with nuanced narratives, made using found objects such as discarded metal, plywood, plastics, rope, and fabric along with paint and pastels.[3]

The subjects of his works range from the allegorical to the abstract, featuring densely textured surfaces with complex designs and recurring motifs of animals and nature. His art also often references the hardship of his own life, emphasizing the marginalized place of African American men and women in American history. Dial's work, stored in an aunt's turkey coop, was discovered in 1987 by William (Bill) S. Arnett, an Atlanta-based collector of Southern African American artists.[4] With financial support from Arnett, Dial continued to make a prolific body of works of increasing scale and complexity.[5]

A Hippo Got a Right to the Tree of Life is an example of Dial's earlier paintings, which focused on themes of nature "to convey the animalistic sense that man and nature are one."[6] It features a hippopotamus in the foreground, partially concealed behind a row of flowers in the background. Both images are used as metaphorical and thematic devices by Dial; together, the hippo, symbolizing an animal with African heritage, and the field in which it grazes represent a memorable evocation of the artist's own heritage and the farmlands that Dial knew and worked in as a child.[7] Dial also created a large body of works on paper with crayon, charcoal, and pastel, beginning in the 1990s. These works from the *Everyday Life* series depict female figures in swirling, dynamic compositions. The recurring motif in this series is that of a female figure interacting with animals such as birds, fish, and tigers, to symbolize the complexities of relationships between men and women.[8]

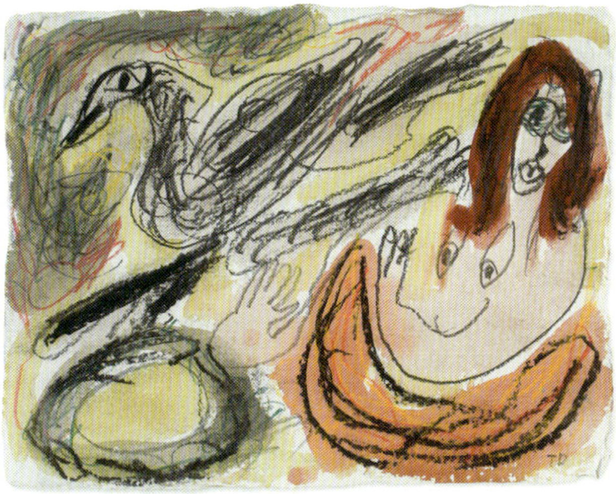

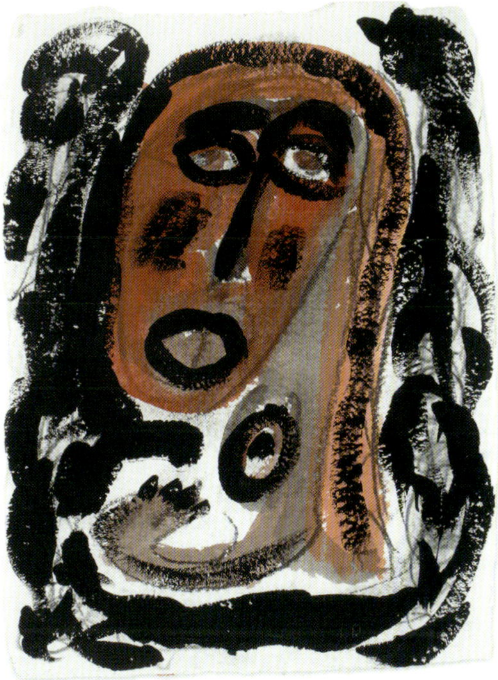

1. William Grimes, "Thornton Dial, 87, Artist Who Turned Castoff Items into Museum Pieces," *The New York Times*, January 27, 2016.
2. Charles Russell and Carol Crown, eds., *Sacred and Profane: Voice and Vision in Southern Self-Taught Art* (Jackson: University of Mississippi Press, 2007), 176.
3. Andrew Russeth, "Thornton Dial, Pioneering Artist Who Channeled Everyday Materials into Intricate Constructions, Dies at 87," *ARTNews*, January 26, 2016, http://www.artnews.com/2016/01/26/thornton-dial-pioneering-artist-who-channeled-everyday-materials-into-intricate-constructions-dies-at-87/.
4. Arnett recalled first discovering Dial's work, which the artist had been storing inside his aunt's turkey coop. He recalled, "I knew that I was witnessing something great coming out of that turkey coop. The man who had created it was a great man, and he would go on to become recognized as one of America's greatest artists. I can't think of any important artist who has started with less or more." "Thornton Dial (Sept. 10, 1928–Jan. 25, 2016)," Souls Grown Deep, January 25, 2016, http://www.soulsgrowndeep.org/news/thornton-dial-sept-10-1928—jan-25-2016.
5. For more information about the relationship between Arnett and Dial, see Roberta T. Griffin, *Abstraction in the Art of Thornton Dial* (Kennesaw, GA: Kennesaw State College, Sturgis Library Gallery, 1995), 6–7.
6. Ibid., 10. The first solo exhibition of Dial's work was arranged by Bill Arnett at the Sturgis Library Gallery in 1990. Bernard L. Herman, ed., *Thornton Dial: Thoughts on Paper* (Chapel Hill: Ackland Art Museum and the University of North Carolina Press, 2011), 6.
7. "I have did [sic] every kind of farming." Interviews with Thornton Dial by William Arnett in 1995 and 1996. For more information about Thornton Dial's imagery and references to his own life and heritage, *see* www.soulsgrowndeep.org/artist/thornton-dial.
8. See Herman, *Thornton Dial*, 139–56.

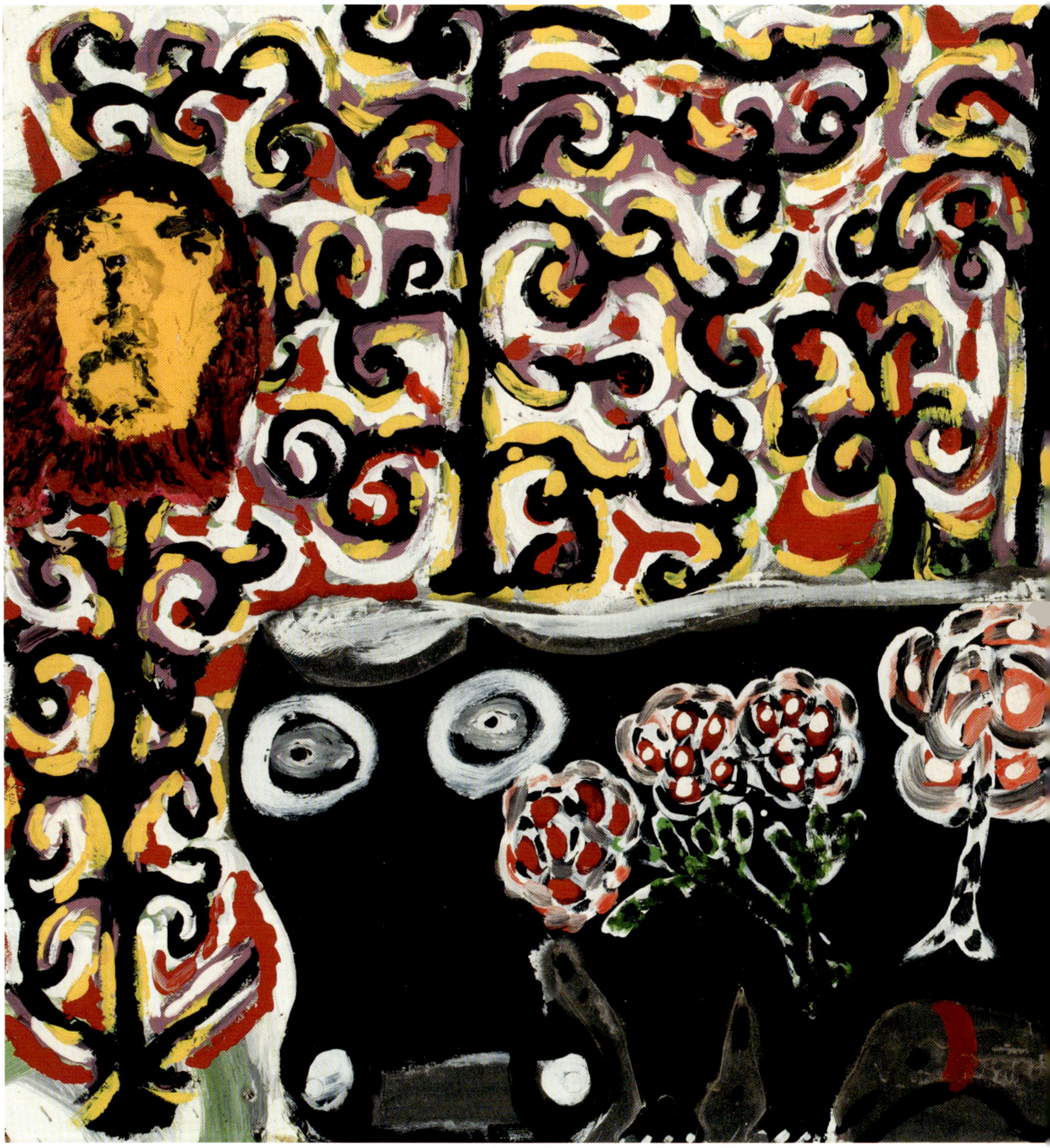

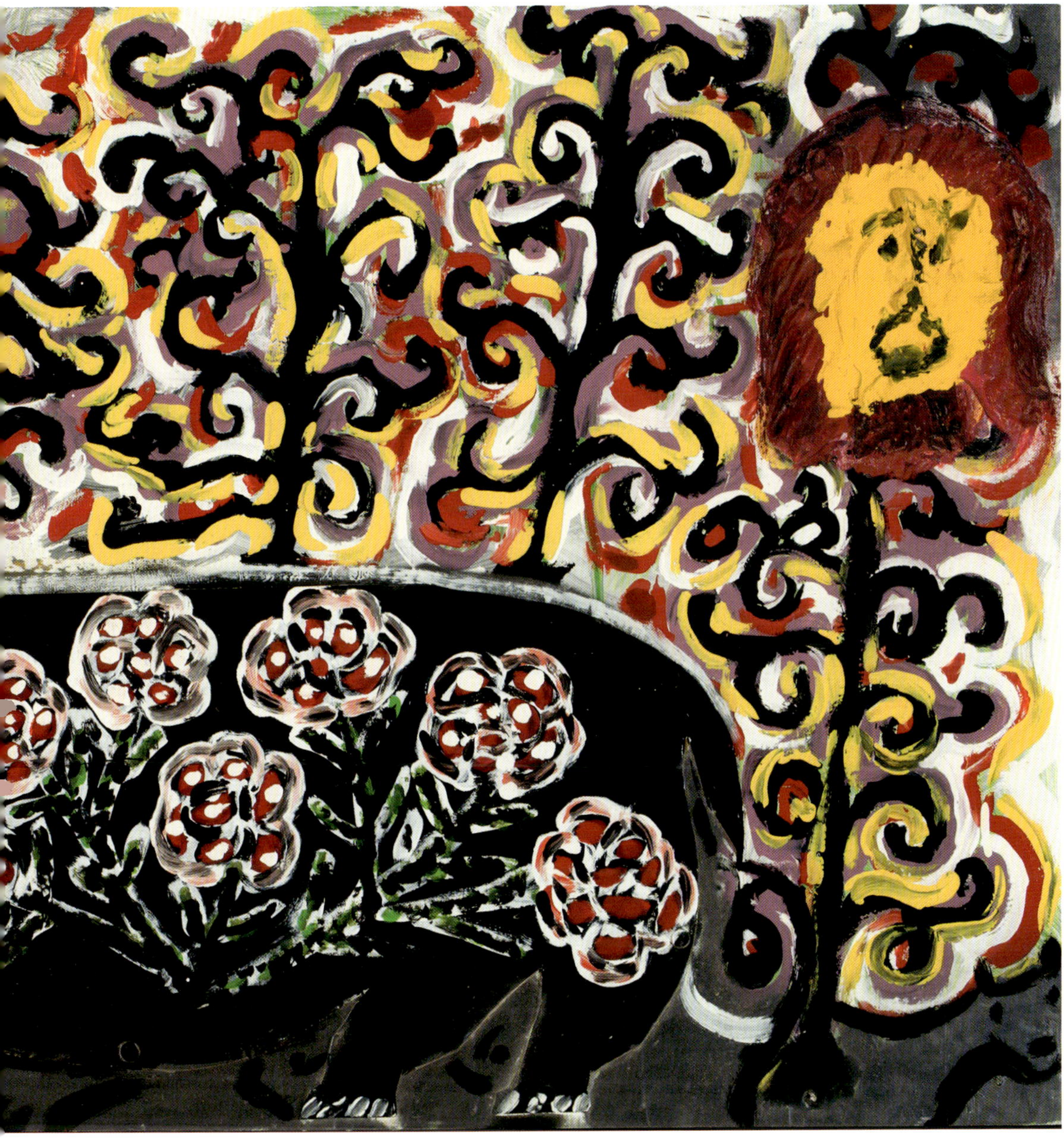

A HIPPO GOT A RIGHT TO THE TREE OF LIFE, 1989
PAINT, CUT METAL, COMPOUND MATERIALS, MIXED MEDIA ON BOARD
24 × 48 × 1½ IN.
2017.037

Thornton DIAL JR.

(AMERICAN, B. 1953)

AMERICAN EAGLE, 1989
(ONE OF A PAIR)
MIXED MEDIA ON BOARD
40 × 48 × 2 IN.
2017.010

Thornton Dial Jr., born in Bessemer, Alabama, and known as "Little Buck," is the eldest of three surviving sons of the artist Thornton Dial. Like his father, Dial Jr. spent time building railroad cars for the Pullman-Standard Company, where he learned the trade of metalwork, a skill that he has utilized throughout his career. Inspired by works of art in his father's backyard, he began his artistic activity around 1986. Today, Dial Jr. acts as the caretaker of his family's property, and also oversees Dial Metal Patterns, the family furniture business. In his artistic practice, he creates paintings, sculptures, and assemblages, conceived in a diverse array of media. His works address a variety of complex subjects and messages, focusing on social conditions, nature, and the African American experience.[1]

American Eagle, one of a pair of mixed-media works, has clear patriotic overtones. It features a bald eagle surrounded by gold stars, set against red, white, and blue stripes. Emblems of national pride, such as the eagle and the American flag, appear in many of Dial Jr.'s works, alongside other iconic images from American culture and mass media.

---

1. Didi Barrett, "Little Buck," in *Souls Grown Deep: African American Vernacular Art of the South*, vol. 2, *Once That River Starts to Flow*, ed. Paul Arnett and William Arnett (Atlanta: Tinwood Books, 2001), 470.

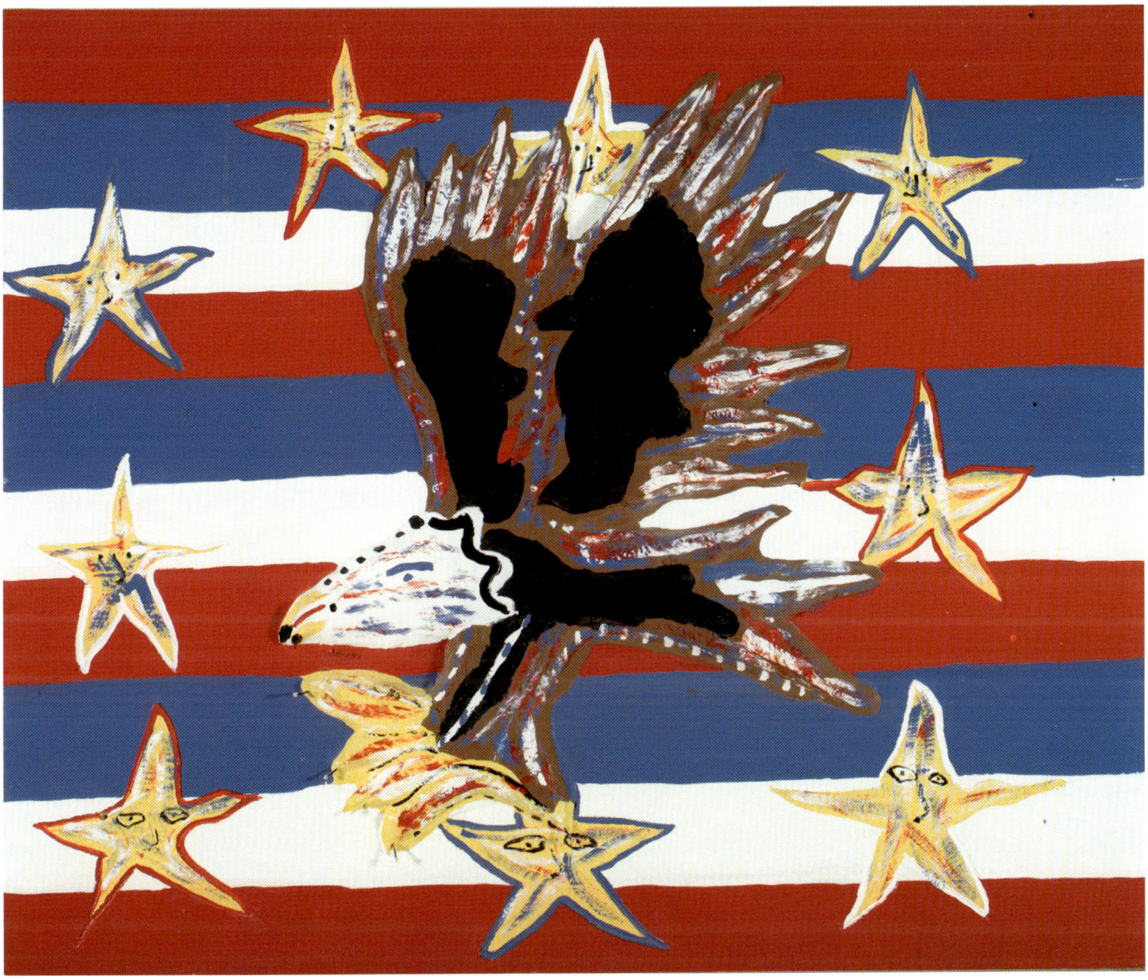

Howard FINSTER

(AMERICAN, 1916–2001)

GIRAFFE, 1990
PAINT ON CUT BOARD;
PAPER ON PAINTED BASE
28½ × 9 × 3½ IN.
2017.011

Howard Finster, born in rural Alabama, gained a popular following as a folk artist and icon through his colorful personality and visionary, proselytizing art. At the age of sixteen, he became a Baptist preacher and proceeded to communicate his religious views to the public by publishing sermons and poetry in local newspapers and hosting a radio prayer show. In 1950, his family settled in Pennville, Georgia, and he began tinkering with different materials and skills, including plumbing, bicycle and television repair, taxidermy, and carpentry. According to Finster, his first vision urging him to create "sacred art" came in 1976. While dipping his finger in white paint, he envisioned a human face on the ball of his finger, and "while I was lookin' at it a warm flash kinda went all over me, all the way down, and it said, 'Paint sacred art.'"[1]

Taking up this artistic calling with enthusiasm, Finster began to create the two-and-a-half-acre environment known as *Paradise Garden* on the swampy land behind his house. Intended as a "Memorial to God," this ever-changing site was composed of walkways, outbuildings, and sculpted constructions made from accumulated cast-off pieces, all covered with apocalyptic, futuristic, and popular culture imagery.[2] Finster became famous for his "sermons in paint," paintings and sculptures ornately inscribed with the artist's own religious proclamations.[3] *Giraffe* and *Rhino* are whimsical animal forms typical of the objects that were displayed on Finster's grounds. The animals, decorated with colorful, repetitive motifs of humans in nature, convey a message of creationism; in the inscriptions, he stressed the distinction between man and animal. Finster followed his signature on both works with "Jesus Saves," aligning his identity as an artist with his identity as a Baptist preacher.

Paradise Garden became a popular tourist destination, and to meet a growing consumer demand, Finster turned his avocation into an enterprise, producing a prolific amount of souvenir art. He obsessively dated and numbered his many thousands of works, inscribing the back of each sculpture with its number and recording the date and time of its completion.[4] In 1994, in ill health, Finster moved away from *Paradise Garden* and the compound fell into disrepair. In 2012, the property was turned in to the nonprofit Paradise Garden Foundation to restore and preserve Finster's legacy.[5]

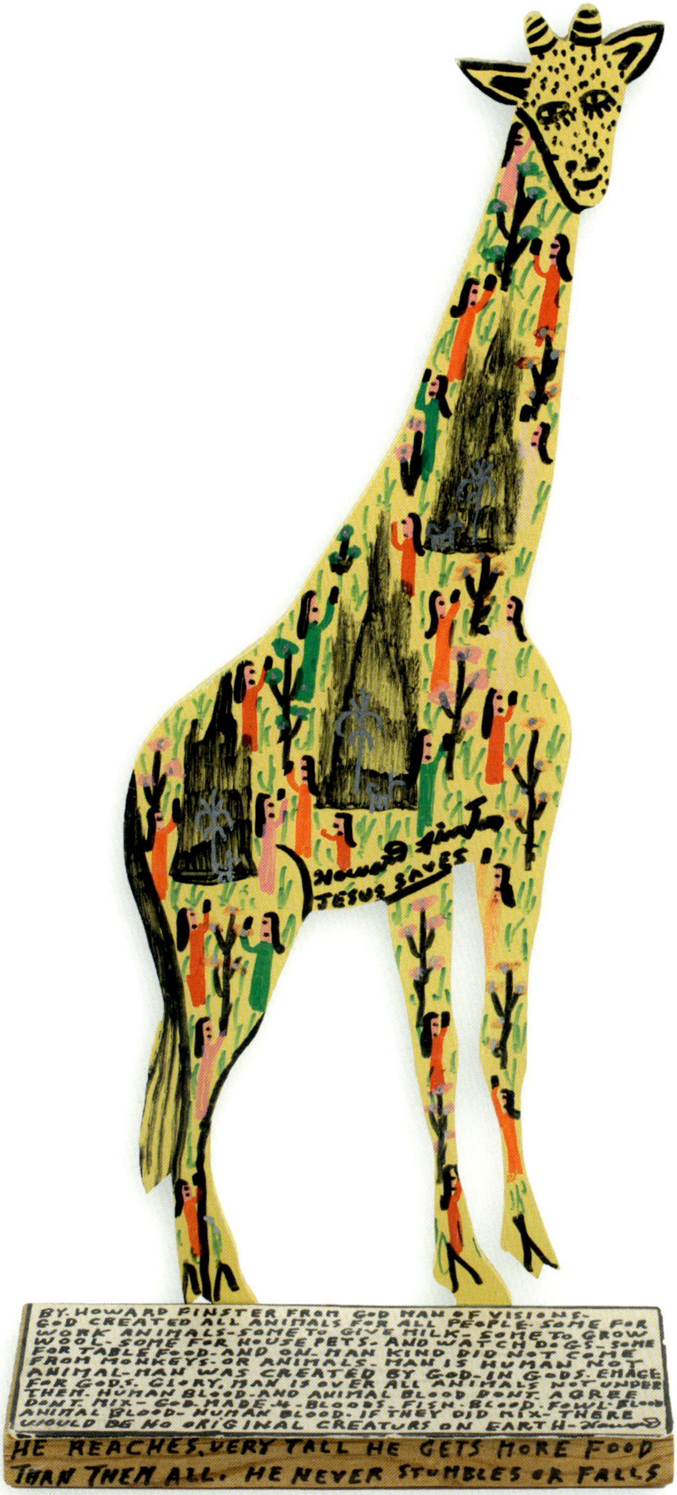
JESUS SAVES
BY. HOWARD FINSTER FROM GOD MAN OF VISIONS-
GOD CREATED ALL ANIMALS FOR ALL PEOPLE-SOME FOR
WORK ANIMALS-SOME TO GIVE MILK- SOME TO GROW
WOOL- SOME FOR HOUSE PETS- AND WATCH DOGS- SOME
FOR TABLE FOOD- AND ON- MAN KIND DID NOT COME
FROM MONKEYS- OR ANIMALS- MAN IS HUMAN NOT
ANIMAL- MAN WAS CREATED BY GOD- IN GODS. EMAGE
FOR GOD.S. GLORY. MAN IS OVER ALL ANIMALS NOT UNDER
THEM. HUMAN BLOOD- AND ANIMAL BLOOD DONT. AGREE
DONT. MIX- GOD MADE-4-BLOODS- FISH-BLOOD. FOWL-BLOOD
ANIMAL BLOOD- HUMAN BLOOD- IF THEY DID MIX- THERE
WOULD BE NO ORIGINAL CREATURS ON EARTH-
HE REACHES. VERY TALL HE GETS MORE FOOD
THAN THEM ALL. HE NEVER STUMBLES OR FALLS

RHINO, 1990
PAINT ON CUT BOARD;
PAPER ON PAINTED BASE
6½ × 15½ × 3½ IN.
2017.012

1. Liza Kirwin, "Appreciation: The Reverend Howard Finster, the Last Red Light before the Apocalypse," *American Art Journal* 16, no. 2 (Summer 2002): 90.
2. Lynda Roscoe Hartigan and Andrew L. Connors, *Made with Passion: The Hemphill Folk Art Collection in the National Museum of American Art* (Washington, DC: Smithsonian Institution Press, 1990), 158.
3. Kirwin, "Appreciation," 90.
4. For a discussion of Finster's abundant production of art, *see* Norman J. Girardot, "Howard Finster," in *Self-Taught Artists of the 20th Century: An American Anthology*, ed. Elsa Longhauser and Harald Szeemann (San Francisco: Museum of American Folk Art and Chronicle Books, 1998), 164.
5. The Paradise Garden Foundation was formed in 2012 after a protracted battle among different groups claiming ownership and the stewardship of Howard Finster's legacy. For more information about the many controversies and overseers involved, see Norman J. Girardot, *Envisioning Howard Finster: The Religion and Art of a Stranger from Another World* (Oakland: University of California Press, 2015), 197–210.

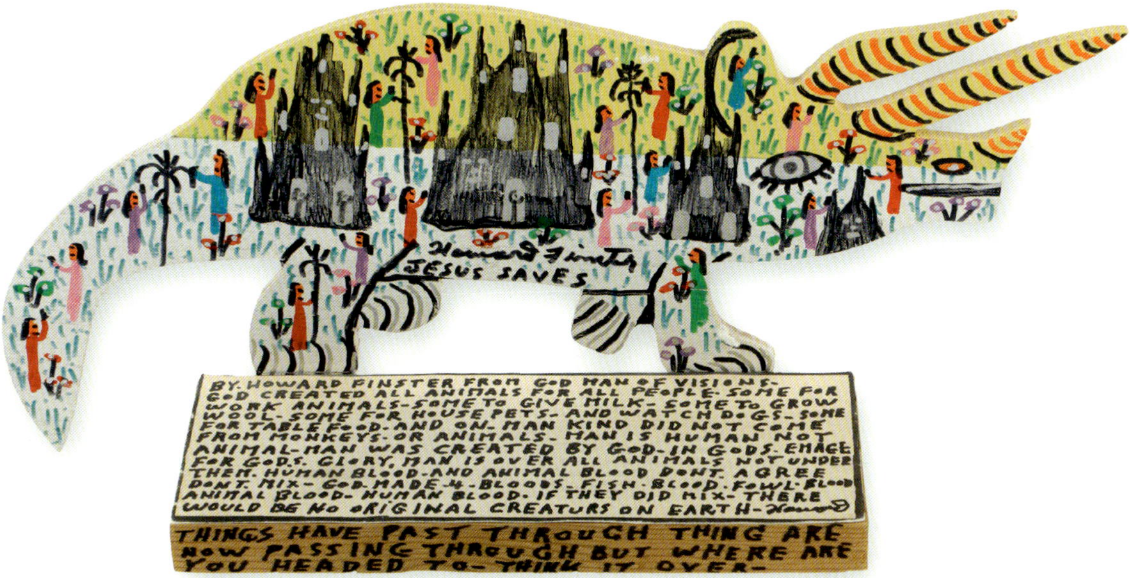
JESUS SAVES
BY. HOWARD FINSTER FROM GOD MAN OF VISIONS-
GOD CREATED ALL ANIMALS FOR ALL PEOPLE- SOME FOR
WORK ANIMALS- SOME TO GIVE MILK- SOME TO GROW
WOOL- SOME FOR HOUSE PETS- AND WATCH DOGS- SOME
FOR TABLE FOOD- AND ON- MAN KIND DID NOT COME
FROM MONKEYS- OR ANIMALS- MAN IS HUMAN NOT
ANIMAL- MAN WAS CREATED BY GOD- IN GODS- EMAGE
FOR GOD.S. GLORY, MAN IS OVER ALL ANIMALS NOT UNDER
THEM. HUMAN BLOOD- AND ANIMAL BLOOD DONT. AGREE
DONT. MIX- GOD- MADE- 4- BLOODS- FISH- BLOOD. FOWL- BLOOD
ANIMAL BLOOD- HUMAN BLOOD. IF THEY DID MIX- THERE
WOULD BE NO ORIGINAL CREATURS ON EARTH-
THINGS HAVE PAST THROUGH THING ARE
NOW PASSING THROUGH BUT WHERE ARE
YOU HEADED TO- THINK IT OVER-

Ray HAMILTON

(AMERICAN, 1919–1996)

STATUE OF LIBERTY, N.D.
PENCIL, INK, AND MARKER ON PAPER
17½ × 24 IN.
2017.013

Ray Hamilton, also known as "R. A.," was most likely born in Hampton, South Carolina. After serving in the US Navy during World War II, he moved to New York City to work on the railroad. Little else is known about his life before he was admitted to a state-run adult home in Brooklyn in the late 1970s. Introduced by a visiting artist to colored ballpoint pens, Hamilton started drawing images from his daily life and memories, as well as his imagination, often tracing the shapes of objects at hand, such as plastic bags, bottles, glasses, fruit, and even his own art tools.[1] He drew in a distinctive, graphic style, using simplified and flattened forms and filling them with dense crosshatching and color. In 1990, Hamilton suffered a debilitating stroke, temporarily losing the use of his dominant right hand.[2]

Statue of Liberty was drawn using pencil, ink, and marker, and depicts the American monument in a bright yellow rectangle surrounded by geometric blocks of crosshatched colors. In *Pigs*, Hamilton outlines the animals with thin lines of ink, and fills them in with solid areas of watercolor; while five of the pigs are neon yellow, the sixth animal stands apart with its more naturalistic shade of pink. *Heads* features silhouetted profiles of three faces, with the exaggerated features and individuality of each face suggesting caricature. *Turky that's giving* is a more complex composition combining groups of human figures and three turkeys, exemplifying Hamilton's highly personal mode of engagement with the figures of everyday life, memory, and imagination.

1. See N. F. Karlins, "Ray Hamilton," *Raw Vision* 24 (Fall 1998): 38.
2. With the intervention of Hamilton's artist-friend Kerrie Schuss, a physical therapist devised a way for Hamilton to draw, wrapping his right hand around pens and pencils secured with thick bands of tape. Eventually, Hamilton also taught himself to also draw with his left hand. Ibid., 41.

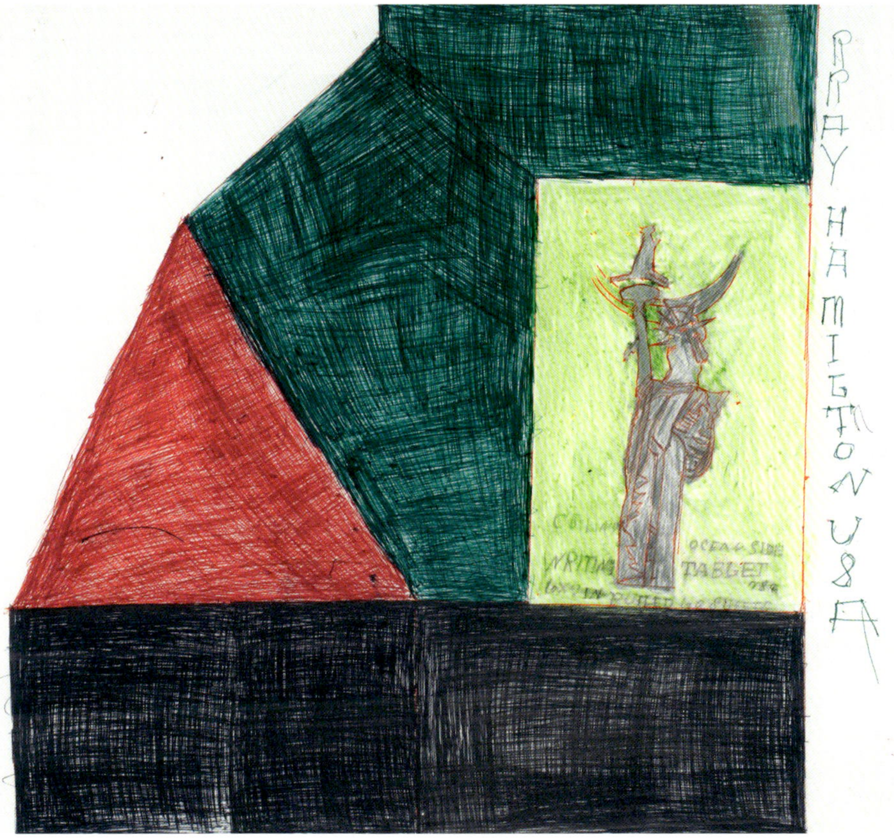
WRITING
TABLET

PIGS, 1994
PEN AND WATERCOLOR ON PAPER
12 × 9 IN.
2017.014

HEADS, N.D.
PEN ON PAPER
17 × 14 IN.
2017.015

TURKY THAT'S GIVING, N.D.
PEN ON PAPER
17 × 14 IN.
2017.016

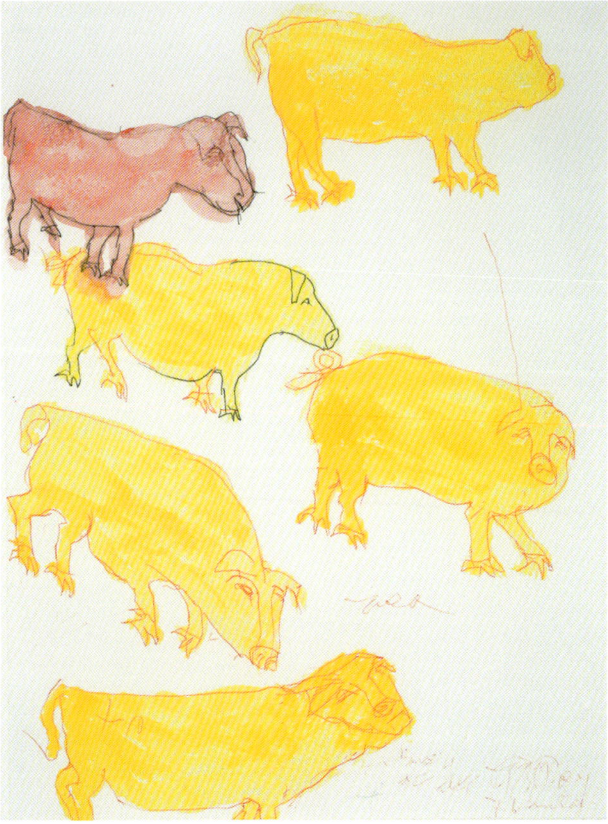

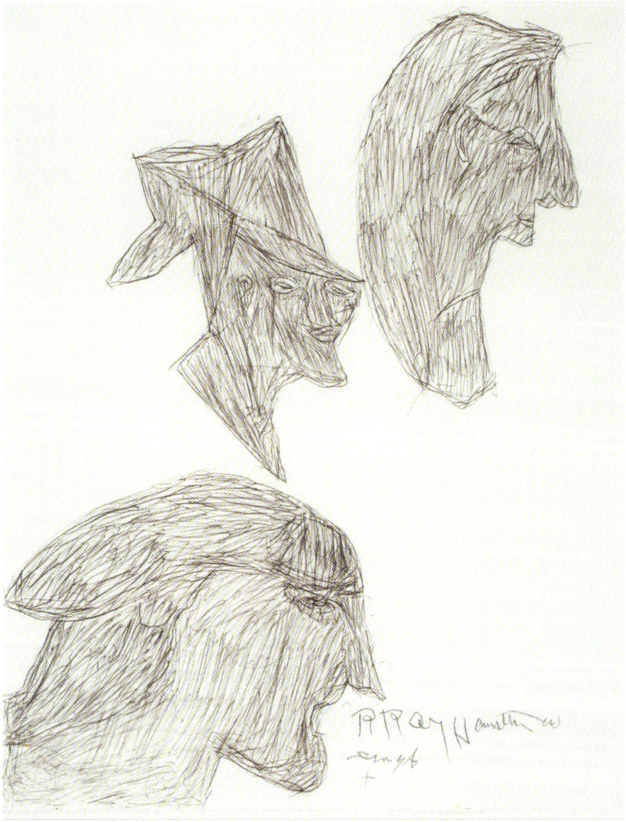

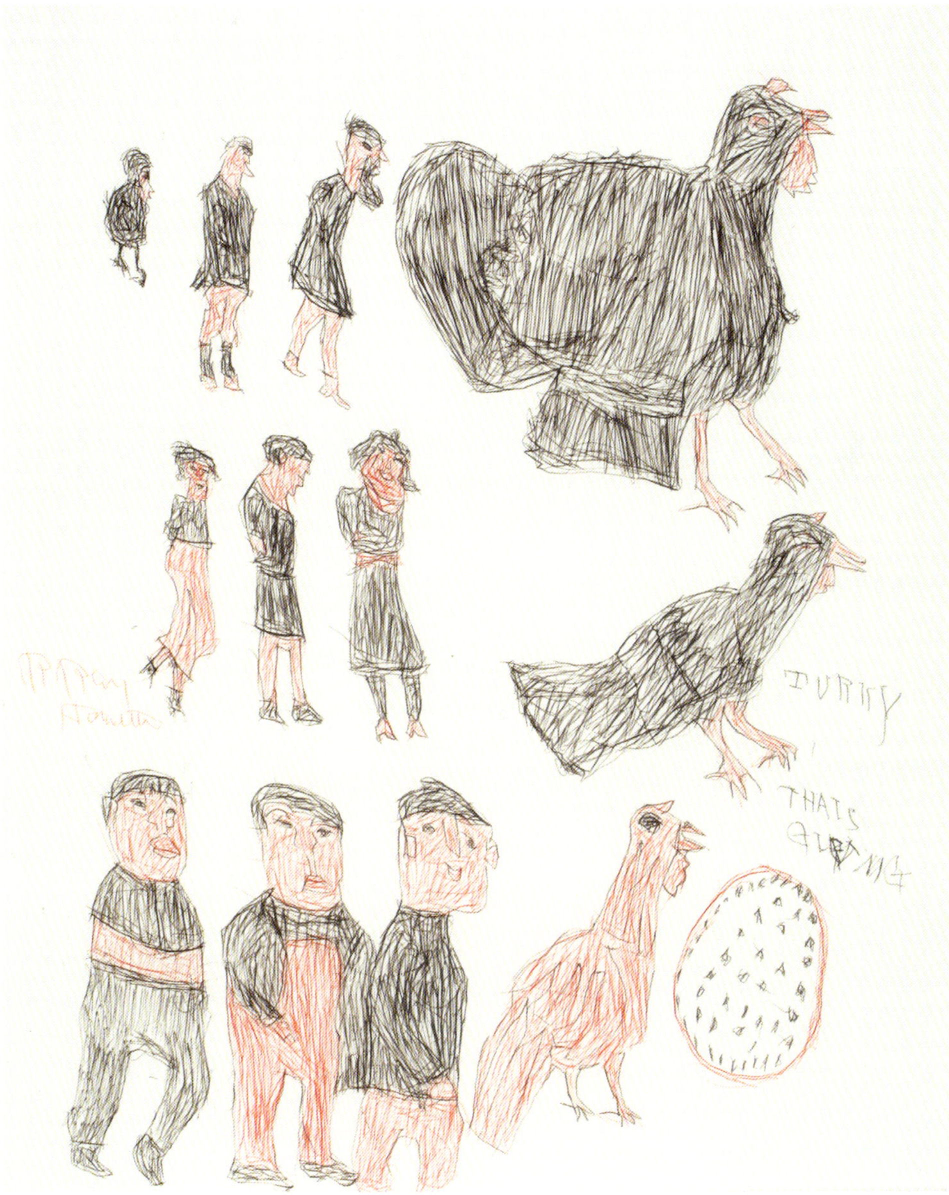
TURKY
THAIS

Bessie HARVEY

(AMERICAN, 1928–1994)

THE SPIRIT OF LOVE, 1985
WOOD WITH POLYCHROME AND MIXED MEDIA (GLASS AND TWINE)
27 × 11½ × 7 IN.
2017.017

Bessie Harvey was born into an environment of scarcity and hardship in Dallas, Georgia, on the cusp of the Great Depression. Married at the age of fourteen, she settled with her growing family in Alcoa, Tennessee. Harvey developed her own creative art practice based on her deep religious faith, and as a relief from the rigors of motherhood and marriage—she had eleven children, along with an abusive, alcoholic husband. In 1972, inspired by visions of the spiritual in nature, she began creating sculptures. Using natural materials, namely tree roots and branches, Harvey brought out concealed faces and figures, finding a way to commune with God. In a 1994 interview, she stated that "to me they were my dolls, they were my freedom from this world, that I could go into them, and I could talk to God, and that the spirit would release me from all of the hurt, and I could hear him speak and talk to me."[1] Her work often reflected her African heritage with African titles and references, and has often been connected to African diasporic religious practices, such as the tradition of *nkisi*, objects imbued with spiritual energy and protective properties.[2]

Harvey is also known for her mixed-media sculptures in wood and clay, in which she embellished found natural forms with manmade objects and personal items, such as strands of her own hair. *The Spirit of Love* is typical of these spiritually meaningful works in its figural form and incorporation of beads, shells, twine, and found wood. The title of this sculpture refers to Harvey's conviction that her artwork "tells of love, and he (God) is love."[3] Harvey was celebrated by her community and lauded by her state as one of its leading artists, receiving the 1994 Alcoa Governor's Award, Tennessee's highest artistic honor. Posthumously, her work was included in the *Whitney Biennial*, Whitney Museum of American Art, New York (1995), followed by a retrospective of her career *Awakening the Spirits: Art by Bessie Harvey*, Knoxville Museum of Art, Knoxville, Tennessee (1997).[4]

1. Bessie Harvey, "God is the Artist," in *Souls Grown Deep: African American Vernacular Art of the South*, vol. 1, *The Tree Gave the Dove a Leaf*, ed. Paul Arnett and William Arnett (Atlanta: Tinwood Books, Schomburg Center for Research in Black Culture, and the NY Public Library, 2000), 160. This essay is based on an interview conducted by Jenifer P. Borum in 1994.
2. For more information on the tradition of root sculpting in the American South and its connection to African diasporic practices, see Paul Arnett, "Root Sculpture: Tornadoes Inside Eggs," in Arnett and Arnett, *Souls Grown Deep*, vol. 1, 126–39.
3. Harvey, "God is the Artist," 160.
4. Kathy Moses, *Outsider Art of the South* (Atglen, PA: Schiffer, 1999), 88.

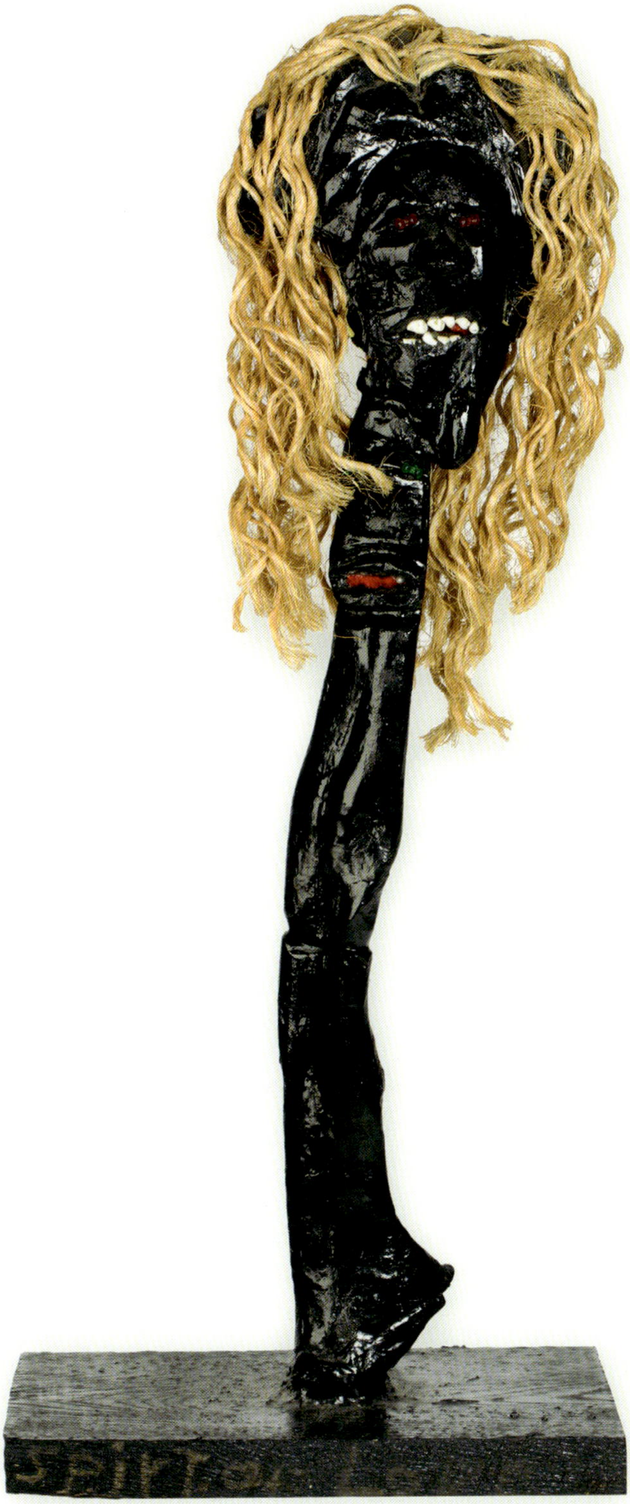

William L. HAWKINS

(AMERICAN, 1895–1990)

HIPPO, N.D.
ENAMEL ON MASONITE
35½ × 41½ IN.
2017.038

William Lawrence Hawkins was born in rural Kentucky. He enjoyed a childhood on the family farm, surrounded by animals, until 1916, when he settled in Columbus, Ohio. In the 1930s he began to draw and sell artworks that reflected a highly personal and rich lens shaped by his life experiences. However, it was not until the mid-to-late 1970s that Hawkins became a painter. His best-known painting style features simplified and graphic depictions of real or fantastical animals, architecture, religious scenes, and historical events, appropriated from a variety of literary, popular print, and other visual resources.[1] Such works, painted in a palette of primary colors, exhibit a dimensional effect of textured brushstrokes, and poured as well as painted surfaces. They also often include Hawkins's trademark: his name, birthdate, and birthplace, prominently inscribed in large block lettering, and surrounded by a hand-painted decorative border. For his first painted works, Hawkins used inexpensive and readily accessible materials: semigloss enamel paint, a single brush, and a plywood ground. Later, when he could afford it, he adopted Masonite as a surface because it did not "suck-up the paint."[2] He would often tilt his panels after applying paint, allowing the pigment to move across the surface, letting the work "make itself."[3] Hawkins would stop working on a composition when he felt that the depicted subject looked "real" and "embodied an energy and life of its own."[4]

Hippo displays many of the strongest characteristics of Hawkins's best animal paintings, which feature both common and exotic, extant and extinct creatures.[5] Within the painted frame, the animal consumes almost the entire foreground space; its massive scale and size further emphasized by confining the giant creature into a small space, with its nose slightly protruding beyond the painted frame. Despite these compositional restraints, the animal appears benign and friendly, with piercing eyes, possibly collaged from a photographic source.[6] The work is titled and signed by Hawkins in his signature style, along with a characteristic stylized decorative border.[7] *Cargur* and *Self Portrait* are examples of the artist's fanciful pencil drawings: in the former, he portrays an invented species of a large, cat-like animal with a curled tail, while the latter is a highly imaginative portrait of the artist, both featuring a decorative border and prominent signature. Hawkins died at the age of 94, leaving behind nearly 400 works that continue to be collected and exhibited at galleries and museums throughout the country.

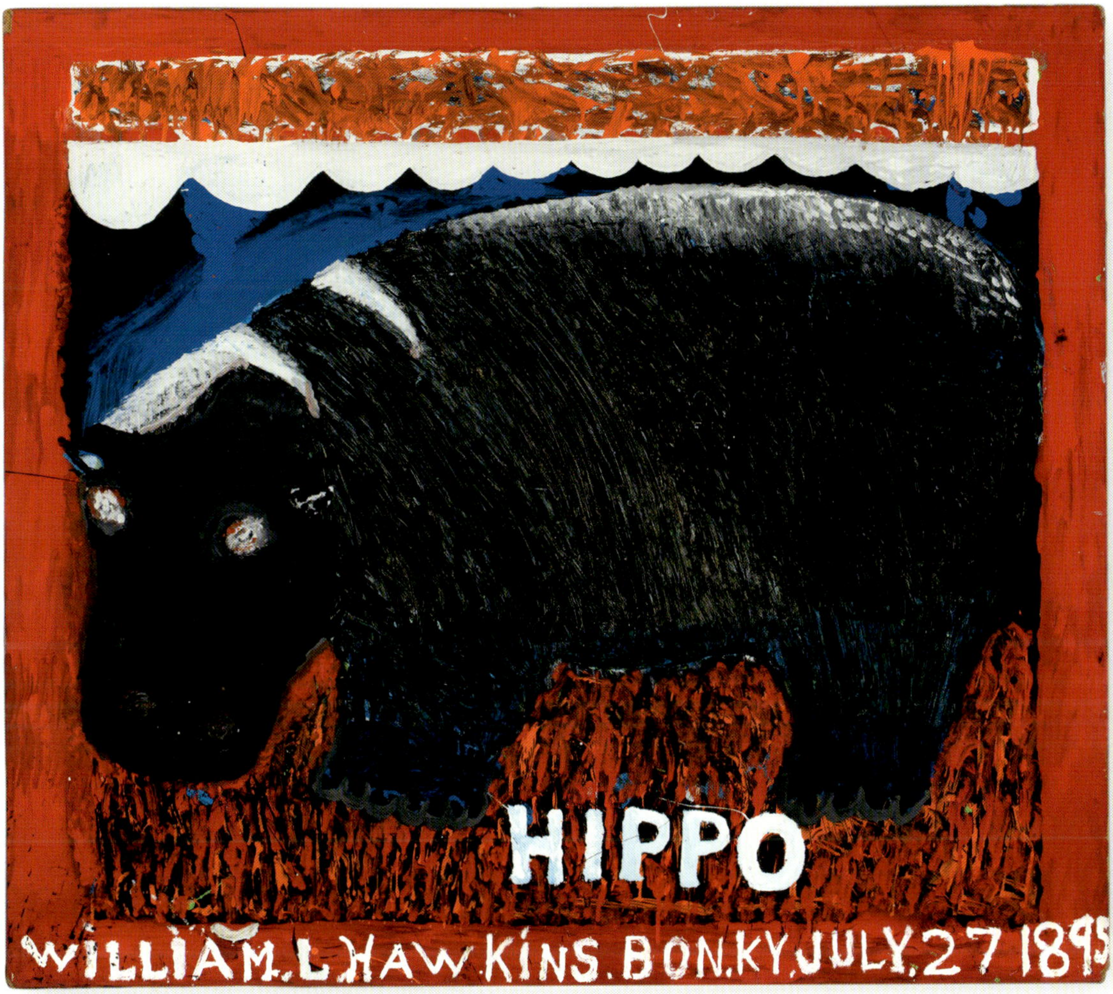
HIPPO
WILLIAM.L.HAW.KINS.BON.KY.JULY.27 1895

CARGUR, N.D.
PENCIL ON PAPER
9 × 12 IN.
2017.018

SELF PORTRAIT, N.D.
PENCIL ON PAPER
12 × 9 IN.
2017.019

1. Gary J. Schwindler, *Popular Images, Personal Visions: The Art of William Hawkins 1895–1990* (Columbus, OH: Columbus Museum of Art, 1990), 9–10.
2. Frank Maresca, Roger Ricco, with Lyle Rexer, *American Self-Taught: Paintings and Drawings by Outsider Artists* (New York: Alfred A. Knopf, 1993), 89.
3. Ibid.
4. Schwindler, *Popular Images, Personal Visions*, 7.
5. Pictures of real or imaginary animals were Hawkins's personal favorites. Ibid., 8.
6. With few exceptions, Hawkins worked from commercially printed images clipped from newspapers, brochures, and posters. "He did not create his own compositions, nor was he a memory painter." Gary J. Schwindler, "William Hawkins," in *Pictured in My Mind: Contemporary American Self-Taught Art from the Collection of Dr. Kurt Gitter and Alice Rae Yelen*, ed. Gail Andrews Trechsel (Birmingham, AL: Birmingham Museum of Art, 1995), 89.
7. For Hawkins, the signature inclusion of his name, birthplace, and birthdate was an affirmation, a mark of his existence, as well as a message to the rest of the world of his special gifts. Mason Klein, "William Hawkins," in *Self-Taught Artists of the 20th Century: An American Anthology*, ed. Elsa Longhauser and Harald Szeemann (San Francisco: Museum of American Folk Art and Chronicle Books, 1998), 172.

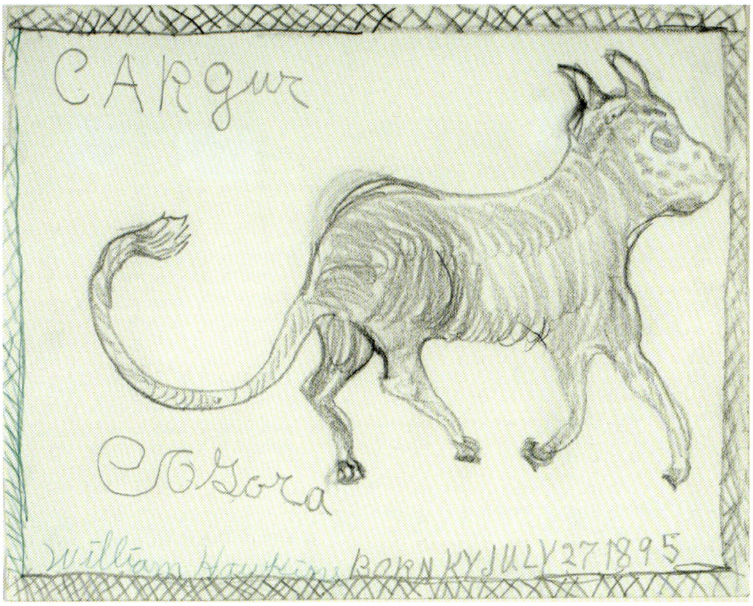

CARgur
CoGora
William Hawkins BORN KY JULY 27 1895

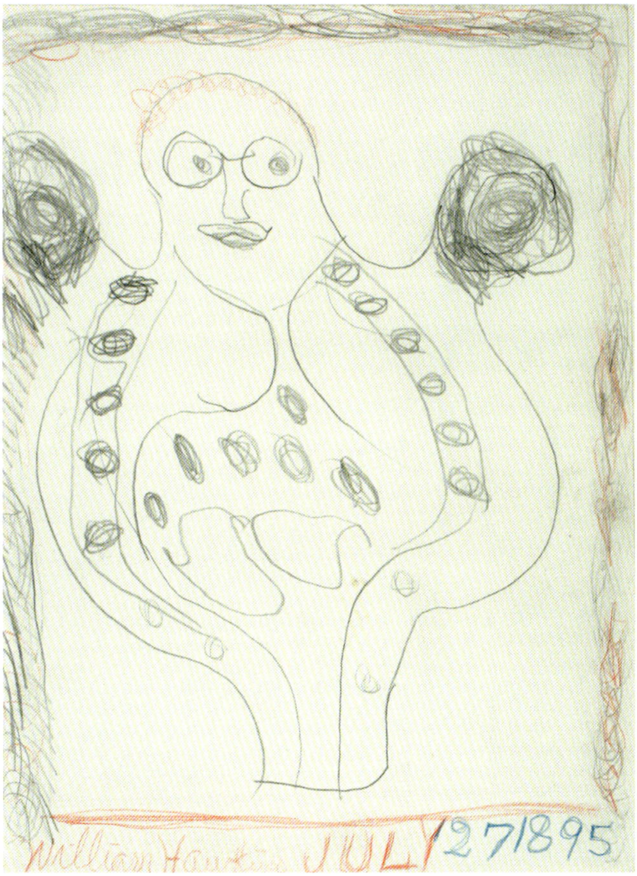

William Hawkins JULY 27 1895

Justin McCARTHY

(AMERICAN, 1892–1977)

CASEY STENGEL ON DUGOUT STEPS 7TH GAME, N.D.
PENCIL, INK ON BROWN CARDBOARD
12 × 8 IN.
2017.020

Justin McCarthy was born in Weatherly, Pennsylvania, into a prosperous family whose fortune waned over time. Shortly after dropping out of law school at the University of Pennsylvania, McCarthy suffered a nervous breakdown. He started drawing during his hospitalization, signing his early work with pseudonyms like "Prince Dashing." He drew continually throughout the subsequent years. His choice of subject matter was eclectic, focusing on any theme that interested him at the moment. He was known to paint in complete empathy with his subjects, occasionally speaking of himself and his chosen historical themes as though there were no distinction between the two.[1] As a recluse, McCarthy took a great interest in popular figures featured in movies, as well as in sporting and historical events.[2] He "reveled in the glut of imagery culled from Hollywood, the tabloids, glossy magazines as well as the inclusion of television into the American living room."[3] He often depicted figures in motion, with elongated and exaggerated arms and legs. Over a career that spanned more than thirty years, he completed many thousands of works. McCarthy lived in the decaying family mansion and sold his works on the premises and at local fairs. In 1960, McCarthy was "discovered" by collectors at an outdoor show, which led to the inclusion of his works in the traveling exhibition *Seventeen Naïve Painters* organized by the Museum of Modern Art, New York (1966–67).[4]

This drawing of the Major League Baseball right fielder and team manager Casey Stengel reflects McCarthy's fascination with sports figures, and records a significant moment in sports history and popular culture. As noted in the inscription, the image was taken from the television screen and documents the New York Yankees' heartbreaking loss to the Pittsburgh Pirates in game seven of the 1960 World Series, which also ended Stengel's career as the team manager at age seventy.

---

1. Jon Ippolito, "Justin McCarthy," in *Self-Taught Artists of the 20th Century: An American Anthology*, ed. Elsa Longhauser and Harald Szeemann (San Francisco: Museum of American Folk Art and Chronicle Books, 1998), 88.
2. Ibid.
3. Ibid., 89, and as noted based on interviews conducted by N. F. Karlins.
4. Gail Andrews Trechsel, ed., *Pictured in My Mind: Contemporary American Self-Taught Art from the Collection of Dr. Kurt Gitter and Alice Rae Yelen* (Birmingham, AL: Birmingham Museum of Art and the University Press of Mississippi, 1995), 128.

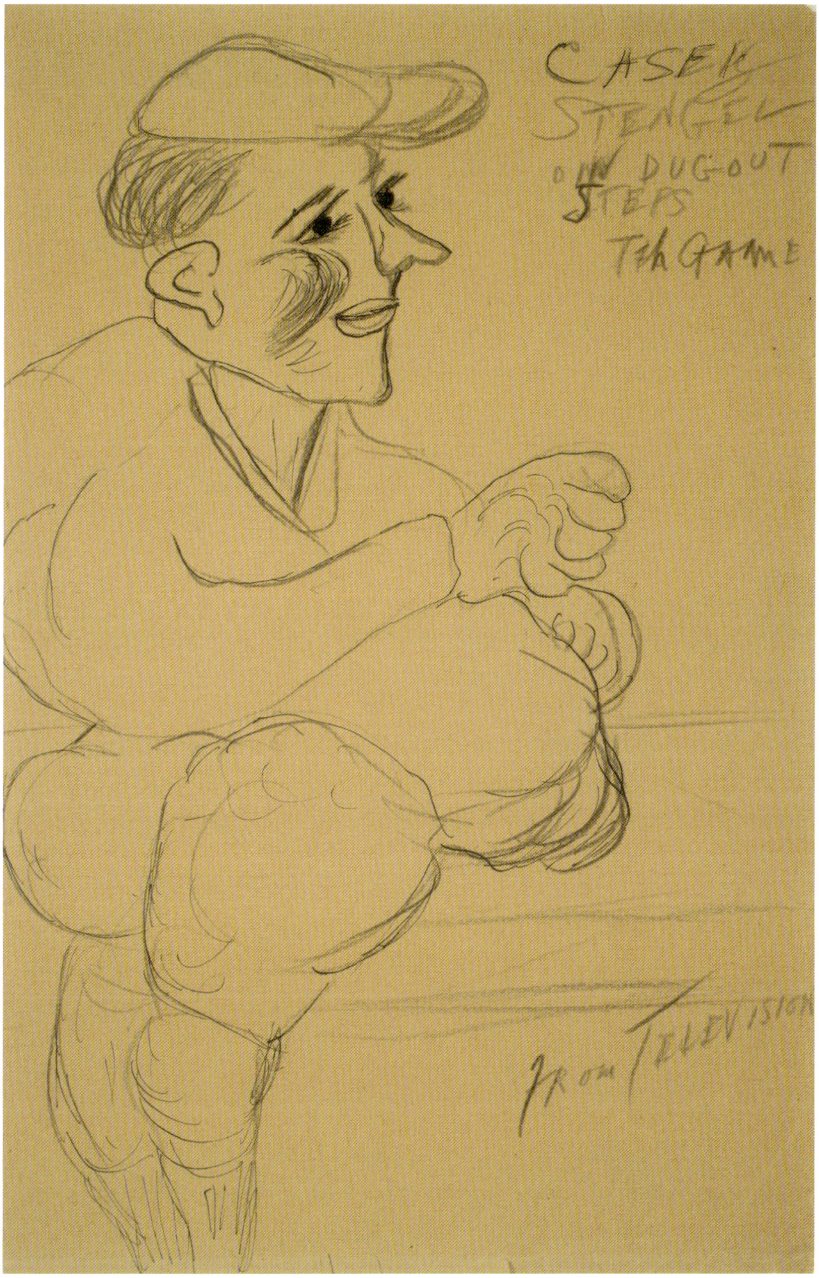
CASEK
STENGEL
ON DUG-OUT
STEPS
TEh GAME
FROM TELEVISION

Malcolm McKESSON

(AMERICAN, 1909–1999)

LET ME SEE YOUR GLOVES, N.D.
INK ON POSTER BOARD
5½ × 4½ IN.
2017.022

Malcolm McKesson was born in Monmouth Beach, New Jersey, to a wealthy New York City family. A Harvard University graduate, he served in the US Army as a lieutenant during World War II, and subsequently pursued a career in his family's pharmaceutical company. In 1961, he withdrew from his business and social life to devote himself to art and to his wife, the poet Madeline Mason. However, the marriage, which lasted forty-eight years, was probably never consummated, with McKesson adopting the role of devoted servant, in awe of what he described as "the strength and wisdom of the female."[1] McKesson kept his creative endeavors hidden, only revealing his erotically toned works after the death of his wife in 1990, when he was well into his eighties.

There is an obsessive quality to McKesson's drawings, both in his distinctive technique of densely accumulating tangles of ink, and in his dedication to a private world that he constructed throughout his adult life. Darkly enigmatic and strongly suggestive of repressed sexuality, his drawings allude to the more explicit themes of his erotic novella, *Matriarchy: Freedom in Bondage*. He depicts a mythological world of doll-like figures of indeterminate age, gender, and identity, who emerge indistinctly from the darkness of scribbled ink to enact courtly rituals and form mysterious relationships.[2] It is a vision, as he describes, of an Atlantean world before men and women were separated and set in conflict.[3] In *Submission*, McKesson portrays a characteristically rounded and shadowy figure isolated in the composition, seemingly devoid of expression or narrative context. *Let me see your gloves* sets the figures into a relationship in which a benign interaction takes on a fraught and sinister air. In contrast, *Figure at Piano* has a more evident erotic charge and voyeuristic quality. McKesson portrays a figure partially obscured by darkness, gazing at a nude, female figure leaning against a piano.

---

1. Tony Thorne, "The Reclusive World of Malcolm McKesson," in *Malcolm McKesson: An Exquisite Obsession* (Surrey, UK: Henry Boxer Gallery, 1995), 4.
2. Ibid., 5.
3. Ibid., 4.

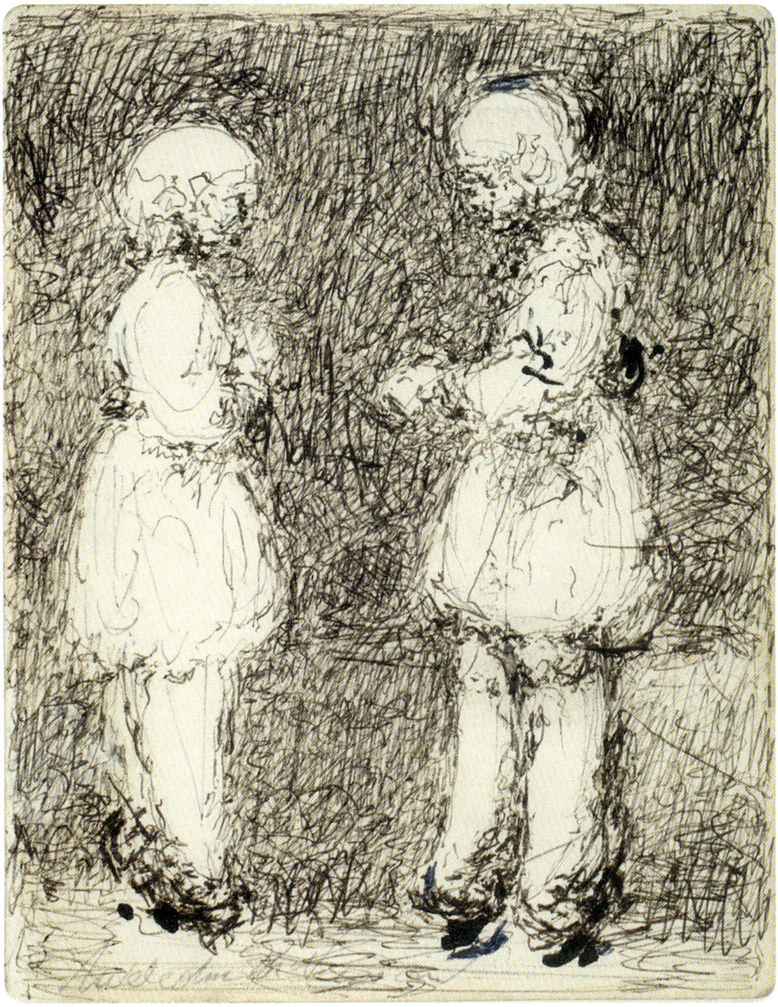

SUBMISSION, N.D.
INK ON PAPER
14 × 8½ IN.
2017.021

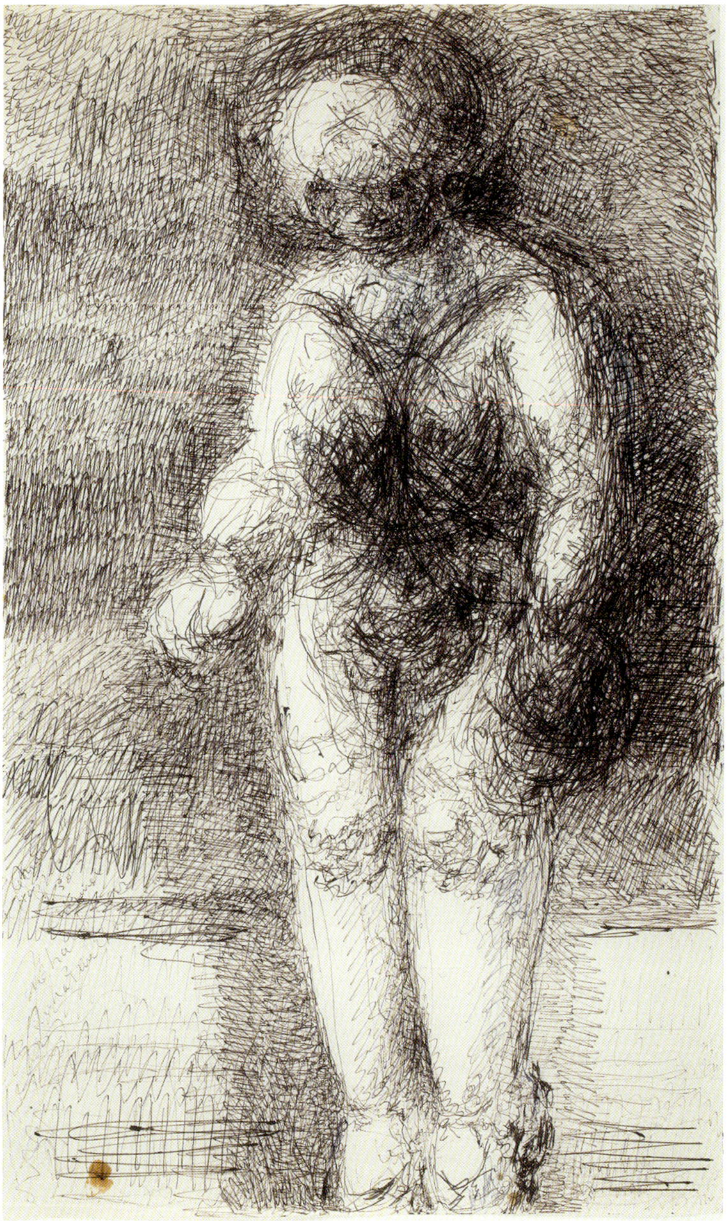

FIGURE AT PIANO, N.D.
INK, MIXED MEDIA ON
POSTER BOARD
13 × 11¼ IN.
2017.023

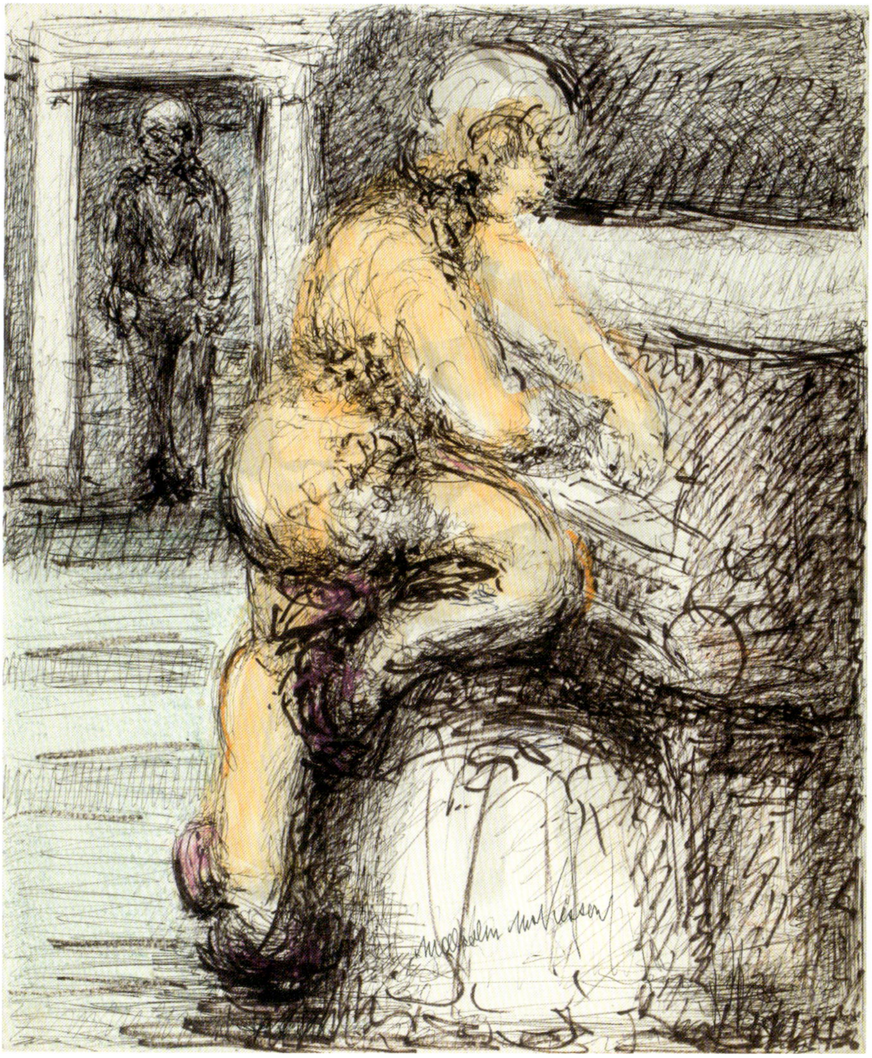

Benjamin (B. F.) PERKINS

(AMERICAN, 1904–1993)

STATUE OF LIBERTY, 1989
OIL ON CANVAS
33 × 23 IN.
2017.024

Benjamin (B. F.) Perkins, also later known as "Big Ben," "Brother Ben," and "Reverend B. F. Perkins," was born in the rural town of Vernon, Alabama. At age seventeen, he joined the US Marine Corps, traveling the world "on secret missions."[1] Upon his return, he attended the University of Virginia, where he reportedly studied "Hebrew history, religion, and engineering."[2] He later served on the security detail of President Calvin Coolidge, and as an airport engineer in Washington, DC. In 1929, he was ordained as a minister in the Assembly of God church, and later became a bishop with the Church of God.

After a divorce, Perkins returned to Alabama and built his own church near his hometown, adorning it with self-created artworks depicting religious and patriotic subjects.[3] The main building was painted with red, white, and blue motifs. As art took over his life, he stopped preaching, built a studio on the grounds, and sought to convey his religious beliefs through prolific imagery. *Statue of Liberty* is one of many images that Perkins painted of this iconic subject, reinforcing his patriotism, his service to the country, and American history.

---

1. Frank Maresca, Roger Ricco, with Lyle Rexer, *American Self-Taught: Paintings and Drawings by Outsider Artists* (New York: Alfred A. Knopf, 1993), 173.
2. Ibid.
3. Perkins fought a seven-year battle with the Church of God, forcing him to create his own congregation known as the Hardine Church of God. Ibid.

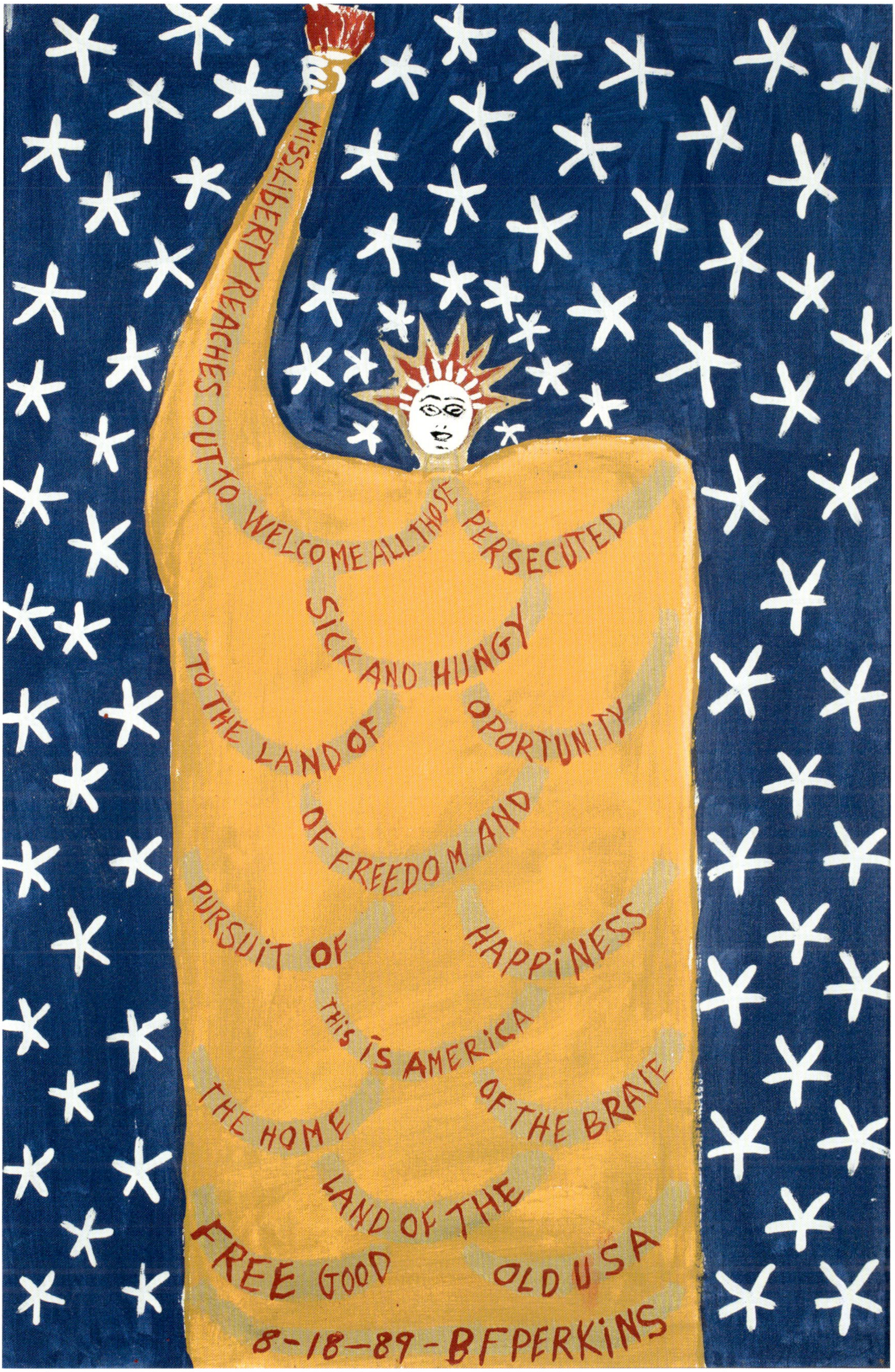
MISS LiBERTY REACHES OUT TO
WELCOME ALL THOSE
PERSECUTED
SICK AND HUNGY
TO THE LAND OF
OPORTUNITY
OF FREEDOM AND
PURSUIT OF
HAPPiNESS
THIS IS AMERICA
THE HOME
OF THE BRAVE
LAND OF THE
FREE GOOD
OLD USA
8-18-89-BF PERKINS

John (Jack) SAVITSKY

(AMERICAN, 1910–1991)

J. JONES MD, N.D.
PENCIL ON PAPER
16 × 18½ IN.
2017.025

John (Jack) Savitsky, known as "Coal Miner Jack," was born in Silver Creek, Pennsylvania, a coal-mining town. At age 18, he began a roughly forty-year career in the mines, until black lung disease forced him to retire in 1959. He readily took to art as a form of leisure and recollection, initially painting with acrylics.[1] Savitsky also drew with a variety of materials, turning to colored pencils, crayon, and pen when advised by a doctor that the paint fumes were aggravating his illness.

Savitsky is best known for charming images that evoke the familiar life, local figures, and landscape of the coal-mining region of Lansford, Pennsylvania. With the assistance of his wife, he sold his artwork at local flea markets before gaining the notice of a wider public. *J. Jones MD* is characteristic of his drawings, depicting a familiar local figure traveling in a horse and cart across a bucolic Pennsylvania landscape.

1. While working in the mines, he drew with chalk on the walls of the mine tunnels, and also sometimes painted signs for local bars, in return for gasoline and cigarettes. Frank Maresca, Roger Ricco, with Lyle Rexer, *American Self-Taught: Paintings and Drawings by Outsider Artists* (New York: Alfred A. Knopf, 1993), 209.

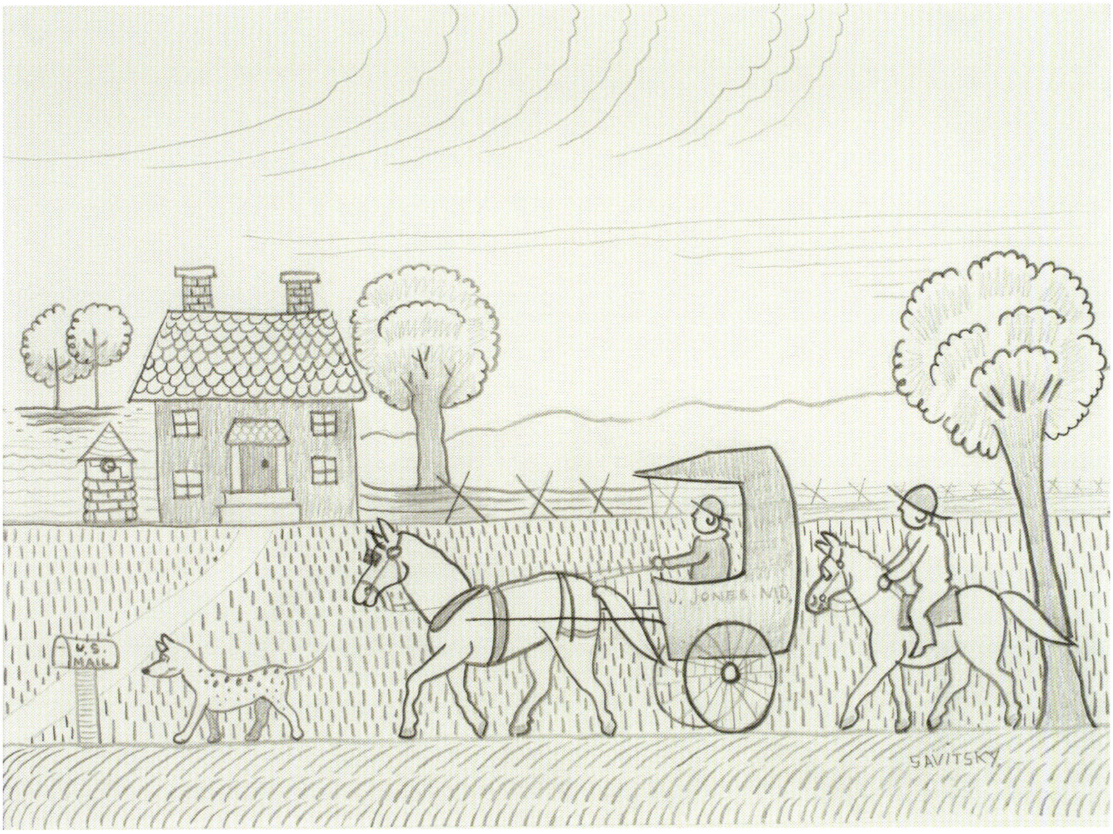
U.S. MAIL
J. JONES M.D.
SAVITSKY

Mary T. SMITH

(AMERICAN, 1904–1995)

FIVE MAUVE HEADS TWO YELLOW HEADS, 1989
ENAMEL ON PLYWOOD
37 × 48 IN.
2017.026

Mary Tillman Smith was born in southern Mississippi to a family of sharecroppers, and endured a difficult life, laboring as a tenant farmer, gardener, and household domestic worker. Smith was born with a hearing impairment, which affected her speech and further limited her educational opportunities. She left school after the fifth grade. From a young age, Smith had enjoyed drawing as a hobby, but her artistic endeavors began in earnest around 1978, when she began to "pretty-up" her yard.[1] Smith marked a fence around her Hazlehurst, Mississippi, home using strips of discarded, corrugated tin, and transformed her yard into a colorful oasis of paintings and assemblages depicting animals, local figures, friends, and family members. Located near a state highway, Smith's artistic environment could be seen by passersby and competed for attention with the billboards that stood above her property.[2]

A devoutly religious woman, Smith expressed her personal relationship with God and imparted her own spiritual revelations through her artwork. She worked with a limited palette of vivid, contrasting colors and broad brushstrokes to create direct, striking imagery, sometimes supplementing her paintings with short inscriptions proclaiming her religious devotion. *Five mauve heads two yellow heads*, a vibrant crowd of unidentified figures, is characteristic of the works that were displayed abundantly on her property. Smith's figures and faces, flattened and frontally oriented, command attention and draw the viewer into her ecstatic artistic vision. In 1985, she suffered a stroke that further impaired her speech and writing, and while she continued to paint, her output of one or two paintings every day was slowed. She died in 1995 at the age of 91, leaving behind a remarkable body of work created in less than twenty years.[3]

---

1. Timothy Anglin Burgard, ed. *Revelations: Art from the African American South* (San Francisco: Fine Arts Museums of San Francisco, de Young, and DelMonico Books, Prestel, 2017), 114.
2. William Arnett, "Her Name is Someone," in *Souls Grown Deep: African American Vernacular Art of the South*, vol. 1, *The Tree Gave the Dove a Leaf*, ed. Paul Arnett and William Arnett (Atlanta: Tinwood Books, Schomburg Center for Research in Black Culture, and the New York Public Library, 2000), 117.
3. Burgard, *Revelations*, 178.

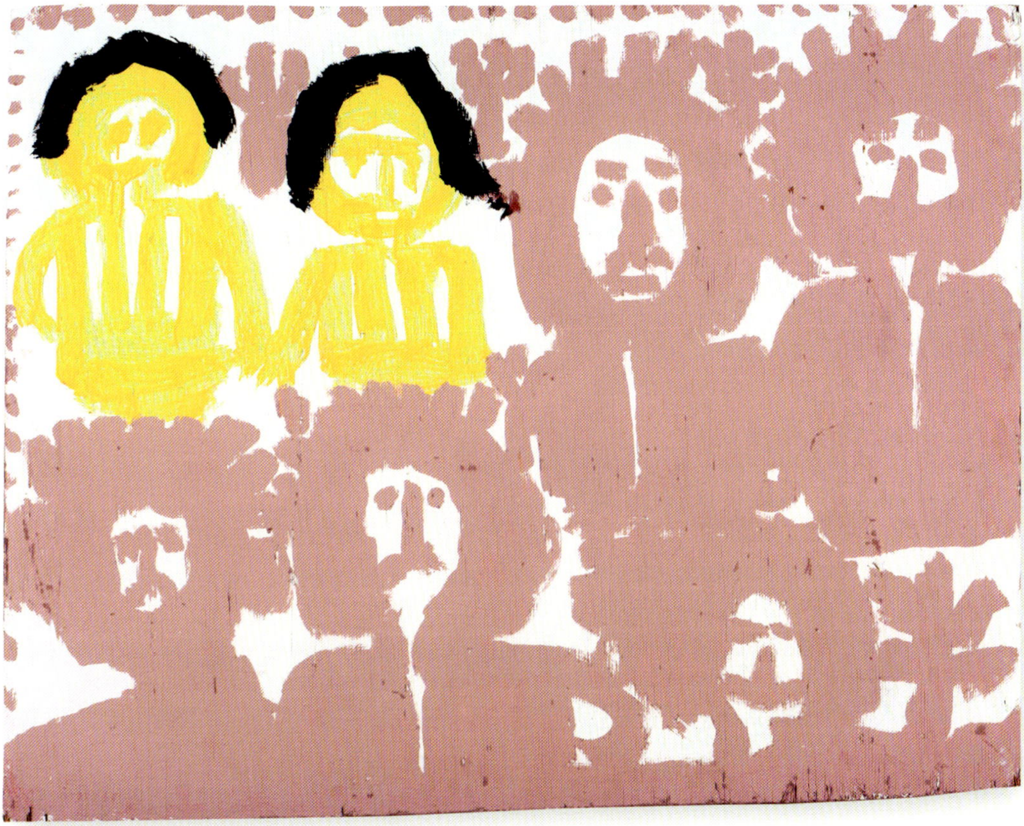

Jimmy Lee SUDDUTH

(AMERICAN, 1910–2007)

SELF PORTRAIT, N.D.
PAINT AND DIRT ON BOARD;
MOUNTED ON FOUND-WOOD SHELF,
SELF-FRAMED
48½ × 36 × 1½ IN.
2017.029

(OVERLEAF)
MANHATTAN SKYLINE, N.D.
PAINT AND GLITTER ON BOARD
48 × 72 IN.
2017.028

Jimmy Lee Sudduth was born in Fayette County, Alabama, and began painting as a child. He had the formative experience at age three of drawing an image on a tree using mud, and finding the image preserved days later. As he recalled: "I got to playing in that old mud hole and painted a picture on a tree."[1] Mud, along with other unusual compounded natural elements, became expressive and trademark materials in his art. He found his pigments in nature, using mud tinted with natural grasses, berries, and other materials, adding sugar or molasses to make the mud adhere to a surface. Foregoing store-bought paint, Sudduth stated: "It was all there in the ground, every color of dirt and mud. I got twenty-three colors of dirt in my yard."[2] The compounded mixture was then applied directly to a surface with his finger in lieu of brushes. When Sudduth became too old to gather supplies in nature, he began using acrylic paint and a single shade of mud, applied with a foam rubber brush as well as with his fingers.[3]

Sudduth's inventive use of natural materials resulted in a variety of textural and surface effects in his self-portraits and images of animals, landmarks, and cities, both real and imagined. His paintings often featured repeated elements, such as the vividly colored and abstracted rows of figures in *Wild Indians*, and the flattened, decorative urban scenery of *Manhattan Skyline*. Sudduth created numerous self-portraits, including this full-length image, in which he represents himself in a hat and overalls with what appears to be a farming implement, reflecting his identification with rural life in Alabama and his upbringing as the child of farmers. In *Statue of Liberty*, Sudduth uses a single shade of mud to form the silhouetted image of the American monument, but the lack of illusionistic depth is countered by the sculptural quality of the surface, with the mud mixture thickly encrusted on the statue's face. The Statue of Liberty appears solidly built and nearly animate in its curving form, an unusually humanizing depiction of the iconic figure.

---

1. William Arnett, "Cutting to the Slice," in *Souls Grown Deep: African American Vernacular Art of the South*, vol. 1, *The Tree Gave the Dove a Leaf*, ed. Paul Arnett and William Arnett (Atlanta: Tinwood Books, Schomburg Center for Research in Black Culture, and the New York Public Library, 2000), 270.
2. Ibid.
3. Alice Rae Yelen, *Passionate Visions of the American South: Self-Taught Artists from 1940 to the Present* (New Orleans: New Orleans Museum of Art and University Press of Mississippi, 1993), 329.

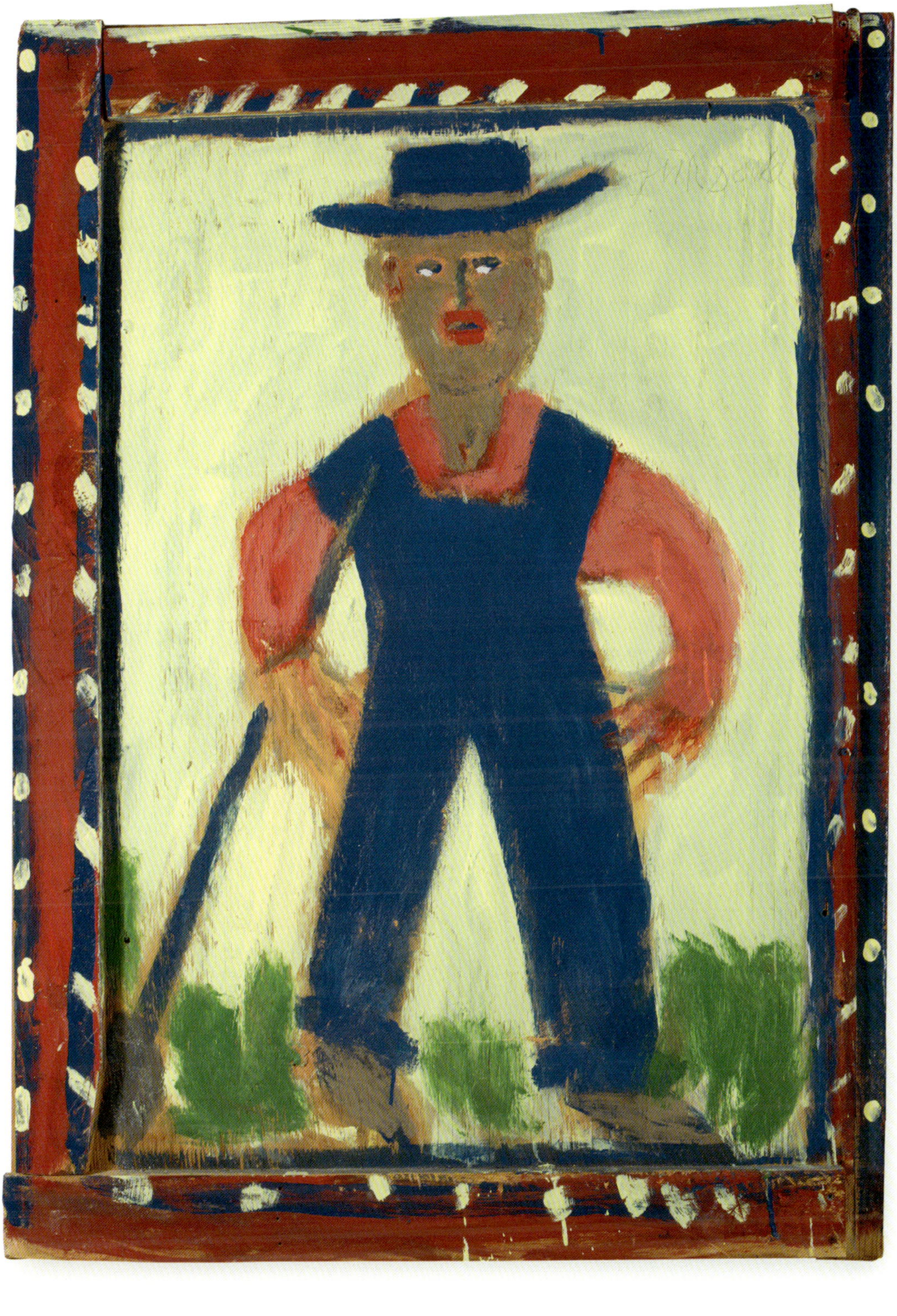

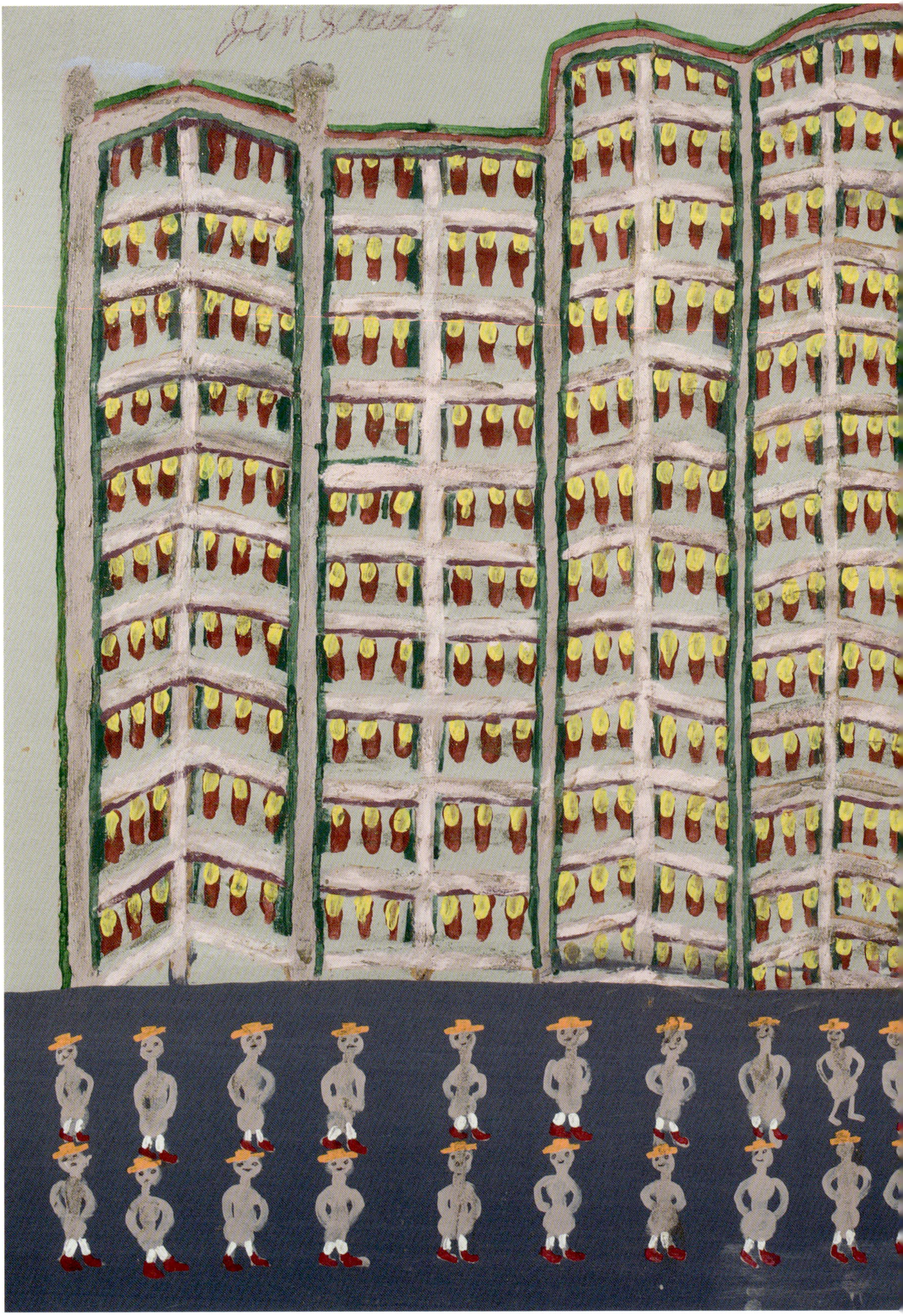

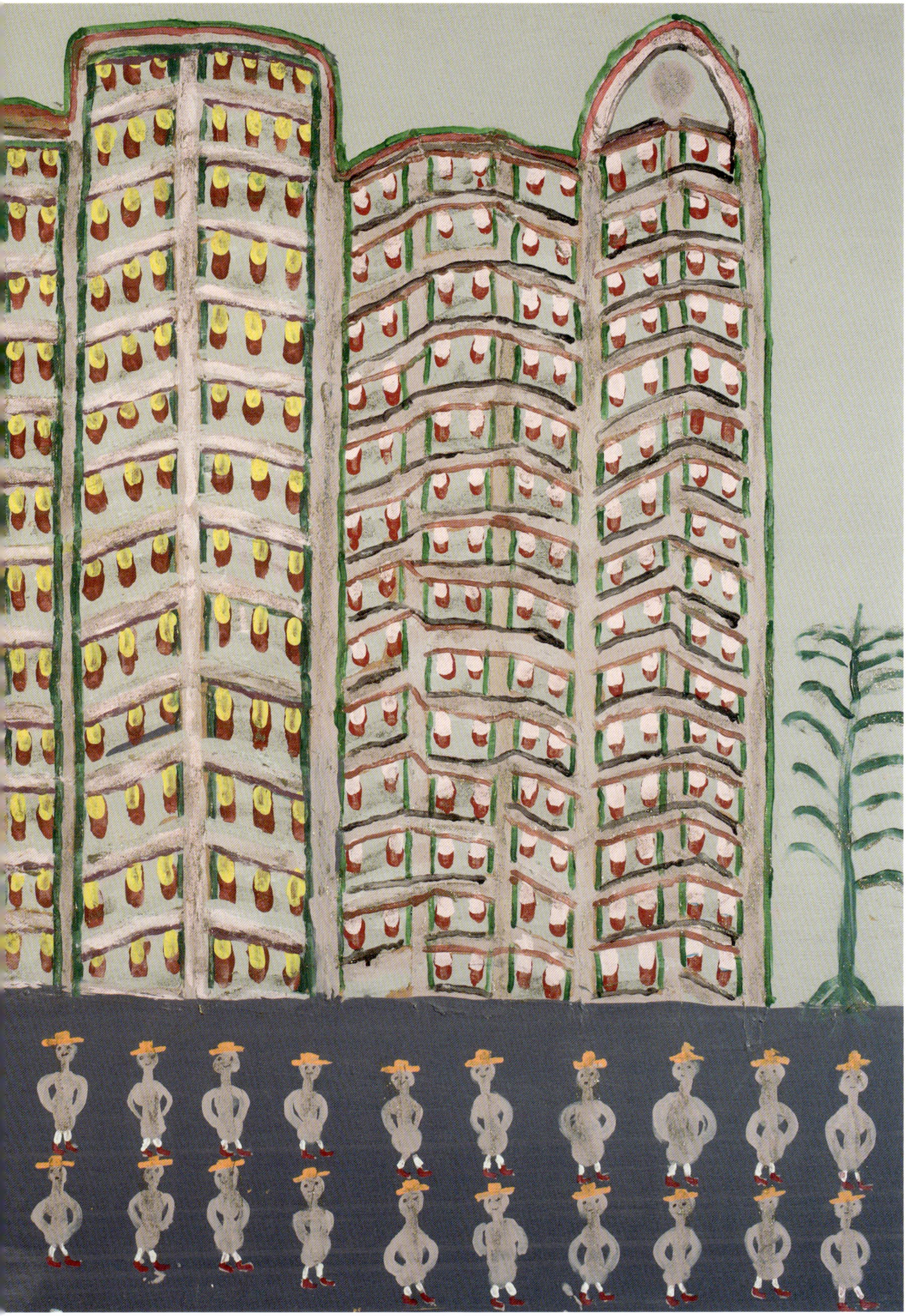

STATUE OF LIBERTY, N.D.
PAINT AND MUD ON WOOD
32 × 24 × 1½ IN.
2017.030

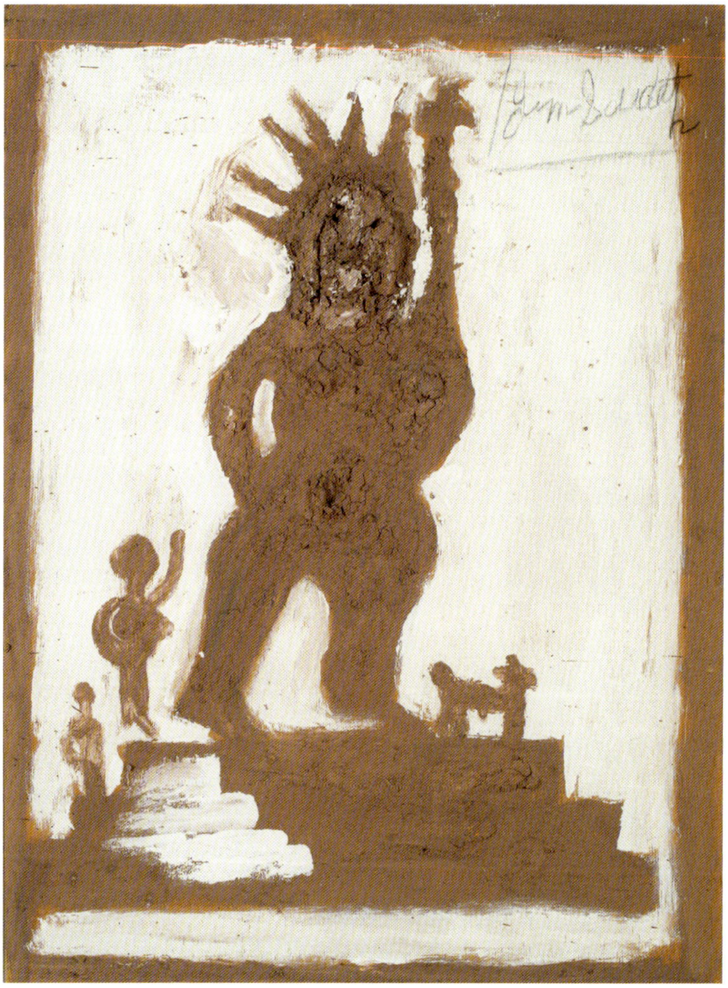

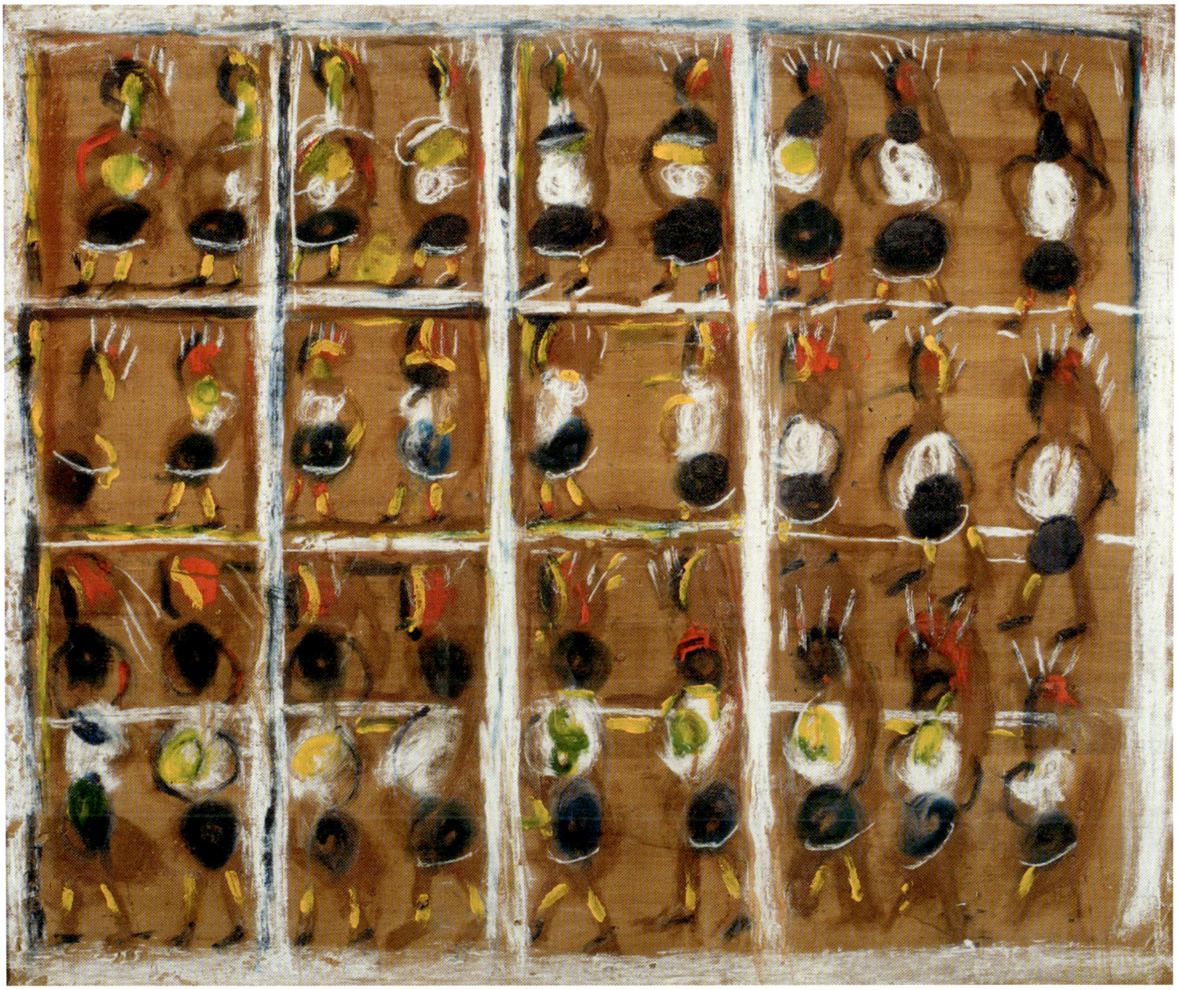

WILD INDIANS, 1989–90
PAINT AND DIRT ON BOARD
47 × 58½ IN.
2017.027

Mose (Moses Ernest) TOLLIVER

(AMERICAN, 1920–2006)

VARIETY FRUIT OF PARADISE, N.D.
PAINT ON BOARD
24½ × 23¾ IN.
2017.032

BLACK WHALE FISH, N.D.
PAINT ON BOARD
18½ × 32½ IN.
2017.031

Mose Tolliver was born in Montgomery County, Alabama. He began painting in the late 1960s after a devastating workplace injury at the McLendon Furniture Factory, where he worked on and off for years. After the accident, and a period of drinking and depression, Tolliver was encouraged to try oil painting by one of his former employers, who offered to pay for lessons. Instead, Tolliver taught himself. He painted on just about any surface—furniture, plywood packing crate sides, and metal—initially relying upon used oil-based house paint before switching to water-based latex paints. At first, he painted birds, flowers, and fruit, later adding self-portraits, people, and other animals, depicting both the objects of everyday life and elements of fantasy.[1] Once Tolliver began painting, he created prolifically, sometimes producing up to ten works a day.[2] Using a variety of inventive and improvised methods, he would hang his paintings on a tree in the front yard of his home to attract the attention of potential buyers.

In *Black Whale Fish*, Tolliver depicts an imaginary "whale fish" in a characteristically graphic style. Nearly filling the composition, the fish, with its contrasting red markings and bright blue eye, is painted with thick brushstrokes over a patterned background. *Variety Fruit of Paradise* is similarly bold and demonstrative of his command of color; Tolliver flattens the forms of bananas, a watermelon, grapes, and other fruit, and arranges these objects across the surface as discrete elements. In declining health, he stopped painting several years before his death in 2006.

---

1. Lee Kogan, "Mose Tolliver: Picture Maker," in *Souls Grown Deep: African American Vernacular Art of the South*, vol. 1, *The Tree Gave the Dove a Leaf*, ed. Paul Arnett and William Arnett (Atlanta: Tinwood Books, Schomburg Center for Research in Black Culture, and the New York Public Library, 2000), 334.
2. Alice Rae Yelen, *Passionate Visions of the American South: Self-Taught Artists from 1940 to the Present* (New Orleans: New Orleans Museum of Art and University Press of Mississippi, 1993), 331.

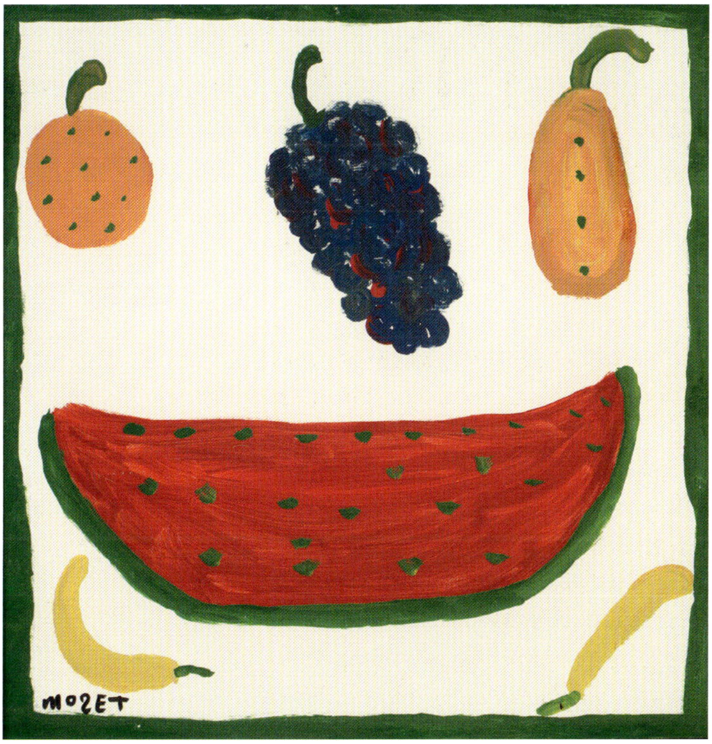
MOZET

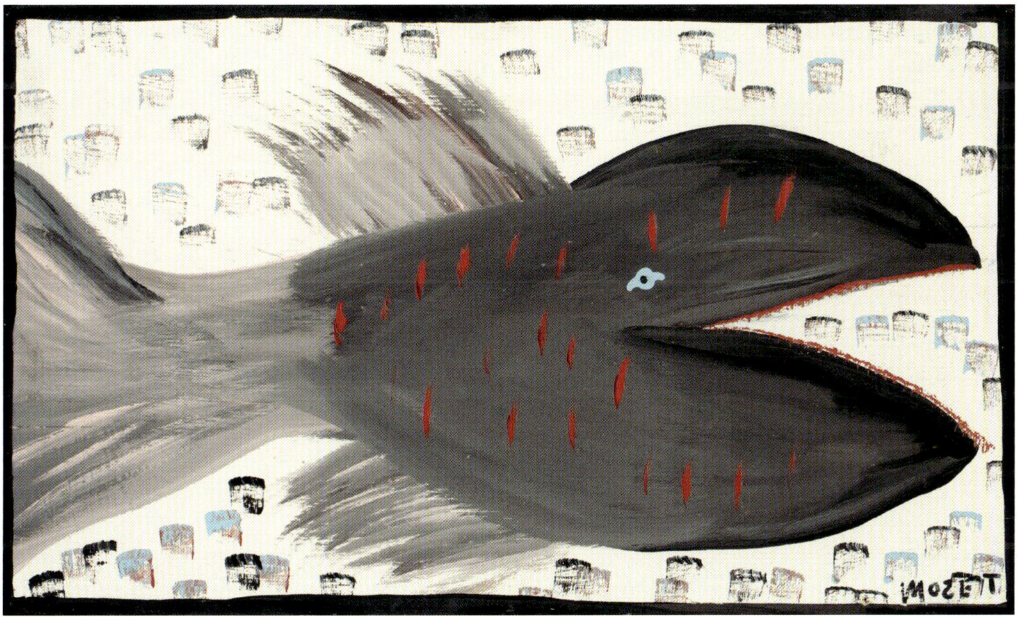
MOZET

Willie (Lamendola) WILLIE

(AMERICAN, B. 1954)

FISH, N.D.
MIXED MEDIA ON PAPER MOUNTED ON BOARD
18½ × 23¾ IN.
2017.033

Willie (Lamendola) Willie, known as "Willie Willie," is a Louisiana-based artist who turned to art making following a career working in a chemical plant. Willie has said, "I'm finally leading an artist's life. I consider myself a contemporary outsider."[1] He is known for creating art from discarded scrap metal, which he cuts with a torch and either paints in brilliant colors or allows to weather naturally. Making frames as part of the art object, he mounts his work on weather-worn wood from demolished barns, and also makes uncut paintings on other materials. Willie hand-built his home in Gonzalez, Louisiana, with reclaimed wood and other scavenged building materials.

Willie's imagery, frequently depicting fish, birds, flowers, and faces, reflects his Louisiana surroundings. *Fish* is a mixed-media drawing of four fish in a painted, weathered frame. Willie continues to work today, but in recent years has adopted a different style and use of materials; his works often feature vividly colored, mask-like faces.

1. "Willie Willie," Gilley's Gallery, June 11, 2012, http://www.gilleysgallery.com/Willie-Willie.cfm?ArtistsID=728.

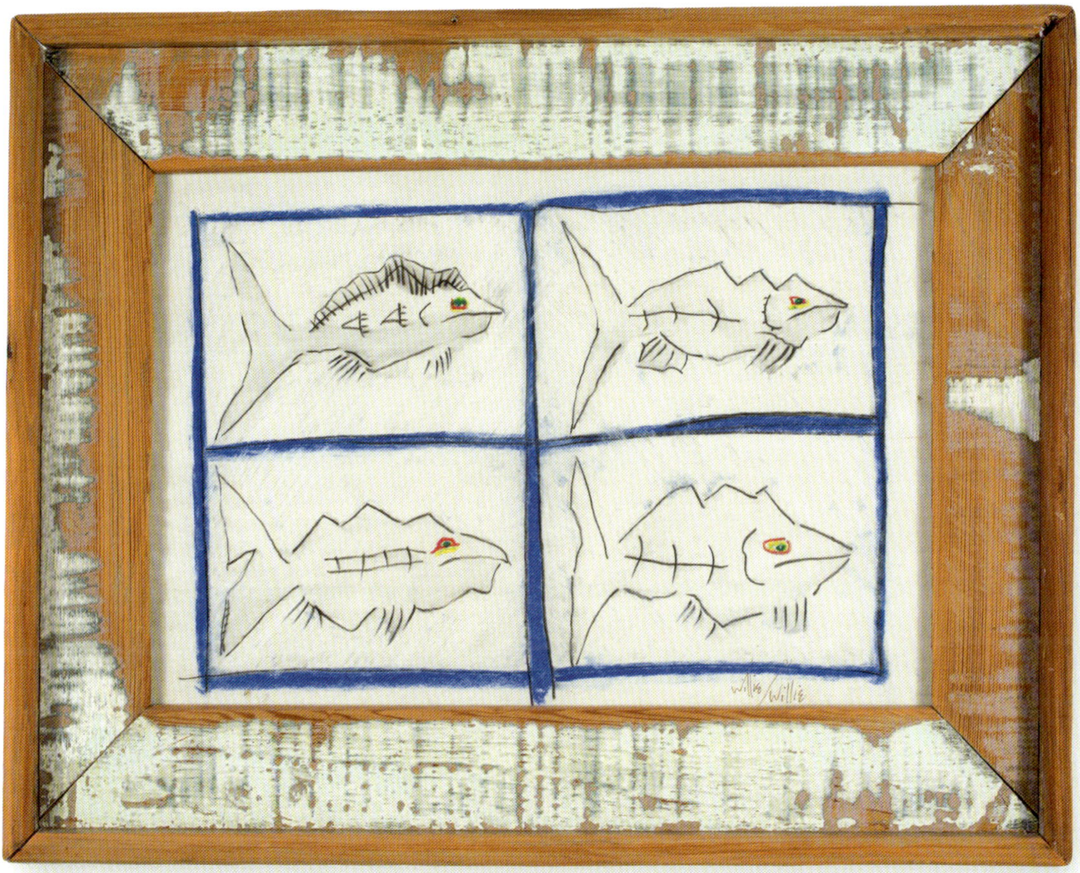

Purvis YOUNG

(AMERICAN, 1943–2010)

CHIEF, N.D.
PAINT ON FOUND BOARD
WITH PAPER COLLAGE
48 × 28½ IN.
2017.034

Purvis Young was born in Liberty City, Florida, and was introduced to art by his uncle. He received little formal education, dropping out of school before reaching high school. While serving a three-year prison sentence for attempted robbery, he began to teach himself about art through books. Upon his release, he began crafting thousands of drawings and placing them in a shopping cart that he rolled around his neighborhood of Overtown in Miami, Florida. Inspired by the antiwar and civil rights protests of the 1960s, he created his own monumental public works, covering the sides of abandoned buildings with "energetic paintings recording the struggles" of African Americans in Overtown's Goodbread Alley.[1] Young made use of found materials, painting or creating mixed-media compositions on scrap board and plywood in an expressionistic style. His observations of life on the impoverished streets of Overtown are transformed in his art through his creative inner vision, bearing witness to the neighborhood's deterioration and the struggles of its largely African American community.[2]

In *Chief*, the figure on horseback, traveling through a colorful and abstract landscape, may allude to the imposing figure of a police chief on patrol, a familiar image during the recurring street riots in Overtown in the 1970s and 1980s. In *Different Horses* and *There's a Figure*, horses—a common motif in Young's paintings—emerge from a chaotic, swirling backdrop suggestive of urban turmoil.

---

1. William Arnett, "Beyond Borobudur," in *Souls Grown Deep: African American Vernacular Art of the South*, vol. 2, *Once That River Starts to Flow*, ed. Paul Arnett and William Arnett (Atlanta: Tinwood Books, 2001), 28.
2. Gary J. Schwindler, "Purvis Young," in *Pictured in My Mind: Contemporary American Self-Taught Art from the Collection of Dr. Kurt Gitter and Alice Rae Yelen*, ed. Gail Andrews Treschel (Birmingham, AL: Birmingham Museum of Art and University Press of Mississippi, 1995), 226. Schwindler describes in depth the physical environment and social atmosphere of the community that Young captured and conveyed in his paintings.

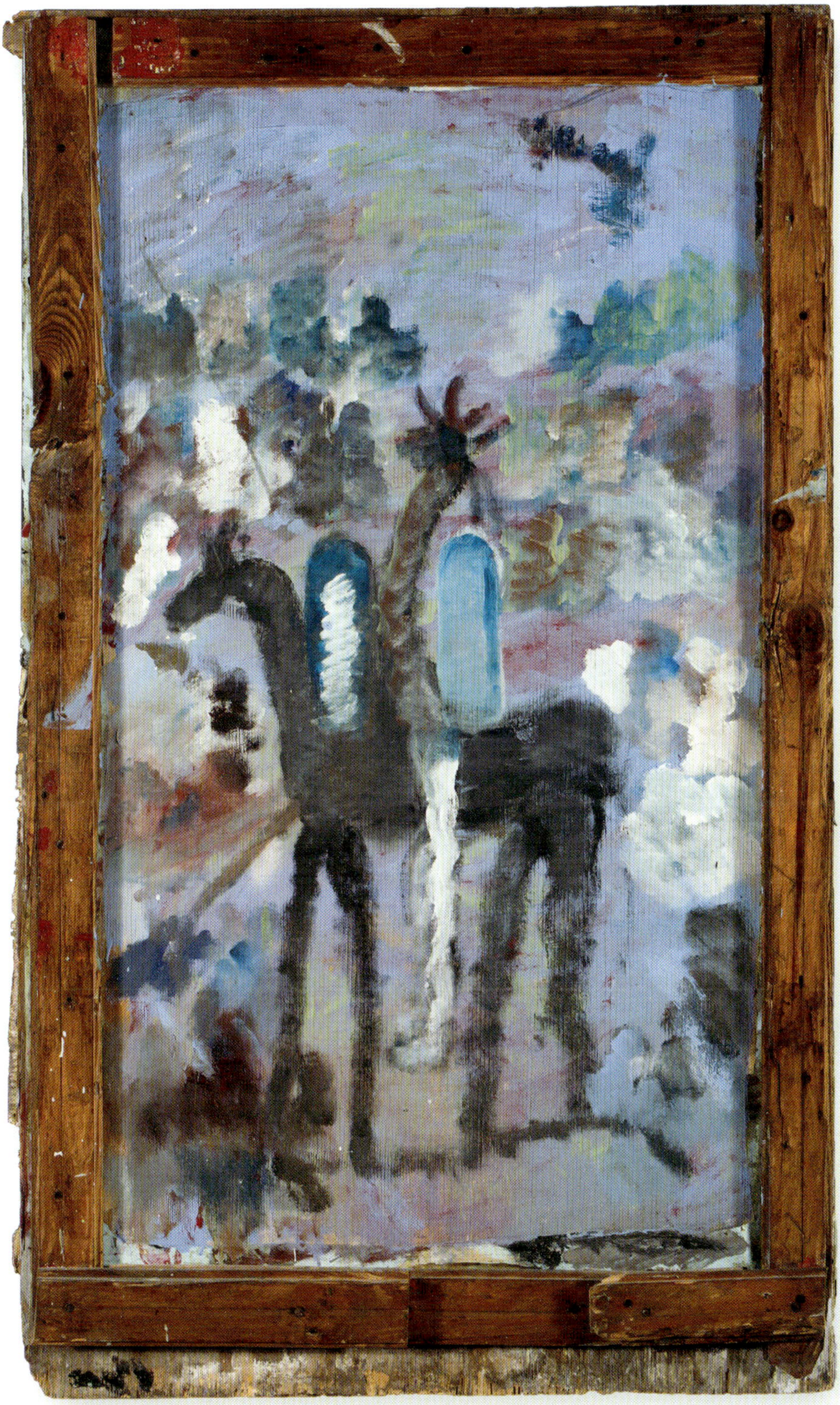

THERE'S A FIGURE, N.D.
ACRYLIC ON BOARD
19 × 44 IN.
2017.036

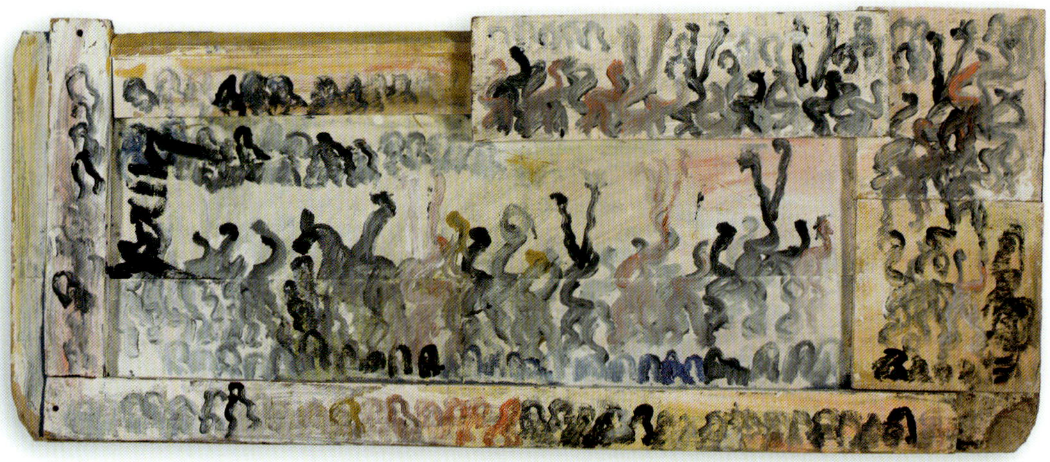

DIFFERENT HORSES, N.D.
ACRYLIC AND MIXED MEDIA
ON FOUND PLYWOOD
24½ × 38½ IN.
2017.035

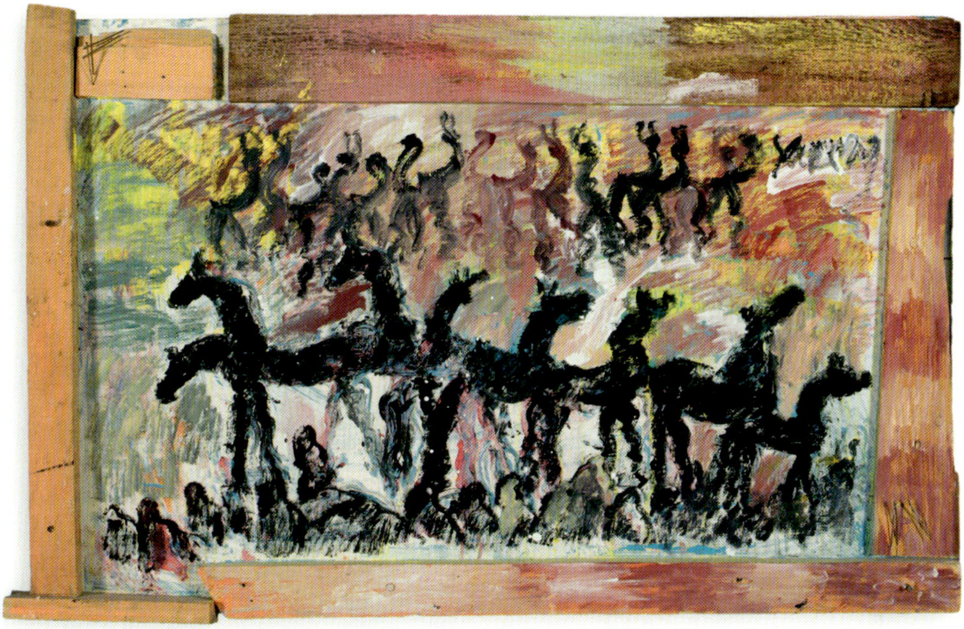

Bibliography

Arnett, William, and Paul Arnett, eds.
Souls Grown Deep: African American Vernacular Art of the South. Vol. 1, *The Tree Gave the Dove a Leaf*. Atlanta: Tinwood Books, Schomburg Center for Research in Black Culture, and the New York Public Library, 2000.

Arnett, William, and Paul Arnett, eds.
Souls Grown Deep: African American Vernacular Art of the South. Vol. 2, *Once That River Starts to Flow*. Atlanta: Tinwood Books, 2001.

Arnett, William, and Paul Arnett.
Thornton Dial, Strategy of the World. Jamaica, NY: Southern Queens Park Association / African American Hall of Fame, 1990.

Burgard, Timothy Anglin, ed.
Revelations: Art from the African American South. San Francisco: Fine Arts Museums of San Francisco, de Young, and DelMonico Books, Prestel, 2017.

Cardinal, Roger.
Outsider Art. New York: Praeger Publishers, 1972.

Cooke, Lynne, ed.
Outliers and American Vanguard Art. Washington, DC: National Gallery of Art and the University of Chicago Press, 2018.

Cubbs, Joanne, and Lynda Roscoe Hartigan, eds.
Let It Shine: Self-Taught Art from the T. Marshall Hahn Collection. Atlanta: High Museum of Art, 2001.

Cubbs, Joanne, and Eugene W. Metcalf, eds.
Hard Truths: The Art of Thornton Dial. Indianapolis: Indianapolis Museum of Art and DelMonico Books, Prestel, 2011.

Dial, Thornton, et al.
Thornton Dial: Image of the Tiger. New York: Harry N. Abrams, Museum of American Folk Art, New Museum of Contemporary Art, and the American Center, 1993.

Finley, Cheryl, et al.
My Soul Has Grown Deep: Black Art from the American South. New Haven: Metropolitan Museum of Art and Yale University Press, 2018.

Girardot, Norman J.
Envisioning Howard Finster: The Religion and Art of a Stranger from Another World. Oakland: University of California Press, 2015.

Griffin, Roberta T.
Abstraction in the Art of Thornton Dial. Kennesaw, GA: Kennesaw State College, Sturgis Library Gallery, 1995.

Grimes, William.
"Thornton Dial, 87, Artist Who Turned Castoff Items into Museum Pieces." *The New York Times*. January 27, 2016.

Hartigan, Lynda Roscoe, and Andrew L. Connors.
Made with Passion: The Hemphill Folk Art Collection in the National Museum of American Art. Washington, DC: Smithsonian Institution Press, 1990.

Herman, Bernard L.
"Charles Benefiel." *Raw Vision* 30 (Spring 2000): 30–34.

Herman, Bernard L., ed.
Thornton Dial: Thoughts on Paper. Chapel Hill: Ackland Art Museum and the University of North Carolina Press, 2011.

Hernández, Jo Farb.
"Sanford Darling, House of a 1000 Paintings." *SPACES*, November 26, 2012.

Hollander, Stacy C., and Brooke Davis Anderson.
American Anthem: Masterworks from the American Folk Art Museum. New York: Harry N. Abrams and the American Folk Art Museum, 2001.

Karlins, N. F.
"Ray Hamilton." *Raw Vision* 24 (Fall 1998): 36–41.

Kirwin, Liza.
"Appreciation: The Reverend Howard Finster, the Last Red Light before the Apocalypse." *American Art Journal* 16, no. 2 (Summer 2002): 90–93.

Lax, Thomas J., and Elizabeth Gwinn, eds.
When the Stars Begin to Fall: Imagination and the American South. New York: Studio Museum in Harlem, 2014.

Longhauser, Elsa, and Harald Szeemann, eds.
Self-Taught Artists of the 20th Century: An American Anthology. San Francisco: Museum of American Folk Art and Chronicle Books, 1998.

Maresca, Frank, and Roger Ricco.
William Hawkins. New York: Knopf, 1997.

Maresca, Frank, Roger Ricco, with Lyle Rexer.
American Self-Taught: Paintings and Drawings by Outsider Artists. New York: Alfred A. Knopf, 1993.

Moses, Kathy.
Outsider Art of the South. Atglen, PA: Schiffer, 1999.

Peiry, Lucienne.
Art Brut: The Origins of Outsider Art. Paris: Flammarion, 2001.

Percy, Ann, and Cara Zimmerman, eds.
"Great and Mighty Things": Outsider Art from the Jill and Sheldon Bonovitz Collection. New Haven: Philadelphia Museum of Art and Yale University Press, 2013.

Puccinelli, Fran, and Ginny Brush
Visions from the Left Coast: California Self-Taught Artists. Santa Barbara: Santa Barbara Contemporary Arts Forum, 1995.

Rosen, Seymour.
In Celebration of Ourselves. San Francisco: California Living Books and the San Francisco Museum of Modern Art, 1979.

Russell, Charles.
Groundwaters: A Century of Art by Self-Taught and Outsider Artists. London: Prestel, 2011.

Russell, Charles, and Carol Crown, eds.
Sacred and Profane: Voice and Vision in Southern Self-Taught Art. Jackson: University of Mississippi Press, 2007.

Russeth, Andrew.
"Thornton Dial, Pioneering Artist Who Channeled Everyday Materials into Intricate Constructions, Dies at 87," *ARTNews*. January 26, 2016.

Schwindler, Gary J.
Popular Images, Personal Visions: The Art of William Hawkins 1895–1990. Columbus, OH: Columbus Museum of Art, 1990.

Schwindler, Gary J.
William L. Hawkins 1895–1990. New York: Ricco/Maresca Gallery, 1990.

Stern, Julian.
"Accidental Magic." *Brut Force*. March 4, 2015.

Thorne, Tony.
"The Reclusive World of Malcolm McKesson," in *Malcolm McKesson: An Exquisite Obsession*. Surrey, UK: Henry Boxer Gallery, 1995

Trechsel, Gail Andrews, ed.
Pictured in My Mind: Contemporary American Self-Taught Art from the Collection of Kurt Gitter and Alice Rae Yelen. Birmingham, AL: Birmingham Museum of Art and University Press of Mississippi, 1995.

Wehnert, Jay.
"Bird and Spirit Root by Bessie Harvey." *Intuitive Eye*, October 24, 2013.

Wehnert, Jay.
"Statue of Liberty by Reverend B. F. Perkins," *Intuitive Eye*, May 23, 2014.

Yelen, Alice Rae.
Passionate Visions of the American South: Self-Taught Artists from 1940 to the Present. New Orleans: New Orleans Museum of Art and University Press of Mississippi, 1993.

Zolberg, Vera, and Joni Maya Cherbo, eds.
Outsider Art: Contesting Boundaries in Contemporary Culture. New York: Cambridge University Press, 1997.

Acknowledgments

This exhibition and publication were made possible by the support of a dedicated gallery team. Special thanks to Tufts Graduate Assistant Elizabeth Kendrick, AG19, who provided research assistance and support for the artists' texts and bibliographies. Thank you to designer Lucinda Hitchcock and copy editor Kristin Swan for crafting these texts into a final and elegant book. Collections Registrar Laura McDonald facilitated the special care, handling, and photography of these new additions to the Permanent Collection with the help of Registrar John Rossetti and Curatorial Assistant Kaelynn Maloney, while exhibitions programming and interpretation was thoughtfully developed by Gallery Educator Elizabeth Canter. Preparator Matthew Murphy deftly installed the exhibition with the guiding designs of Jacob Dyrenforth of Show Shop Design and David Hollely of Hollely | Design Collective. The Tufts University Art Galleries extend our gratitude to Tufts University President Anthony Monaco, Dean of Arts and Sciences James Glaser, and Dean of the Arts Nancy Bauer for continued and unwavering support.

Tufts University Art Galleries

Tisch Family Gallery
Aidekman Arts Center
40 Talbot Avenue
Medford, MA 02155
artgallery.tufts.edu

All work is from the Tufts University Permanent Collection, Gift of Andrew and Linda Safran.

This catalogue is published by Tufts University Art Galleries on the occasion of the exhibition *Expressions Unbound: American Outsider Art from the Andrew and Linda Safran Collection*.

On view August 29 through December 16, 2018.

Cover:
William L. Hawkins, *Hippo*, n.d., enamel on masonite, Tufts University Permanent Collection, Gift of Andrew and Linda Safran. 2017.038

Photography Steve Briggs
Book design Lucinda Hitchcock
Typefaces Sectra, Source Code
Copyediting Kristin Swan
Proofreading Elissa Greisz
Printing die Keure Printing, Brugge, Belgium

ISBN: 978-1-880593-03-5
Library of Congress Number: 2018950175

Printed in Belgium